THE TRUTH SHALL SET YOU FREE

And what I learned in this lifetime.

By Edward J. Evers

THE TRUTH SHALL SET YOU FREE

© 2015 by Edward J. Evers

Published by:
Double E Press
ejevers@att.net

First Printing, 2015

Printed in the United State of America

ISBN: 978-1512320503

Disclaimer

The information in this book is not intended or implied to be a substitute for professional medical advice, diagnosis or treatment. All content, including text, graphics, images and information, contained on or available through this book is for general information purposes only.

The author makes no representation and assumes no responsibility for the accuracy of information contained in or made available through the information contained in this book.

You are encouraged to confirm any information obtained from or through the information in this book with other sources, and review all information regarding any medical condition or treatment with your physician.

Contents

PREFACE

I have been searching for truths nearly every day of my life. I am now eighty two years old, and like most people I still have many questions.

Some of the words I have documented here came from the many studies I have undertaken for the past 40 to 45 years. Some came from a few very wise people I met, some came to me in the middle of some of my many sleepless nights sitting on the edge of my bed at three AM in the morning and some came from my own experiences.

Most of the unusual events I experienced in life seemed very real, and most make perfect sense to me. Perhaps they will to you also.

I'm not including all my beliefs and theories in this book, as some are a bit too bizarre.

If this book goes well, perhaps I will venture an attempt to take you beyond all reason and sanity with a truly bizarre sequel. While I am on the subject of bizarre, since some of the subject matter in my book came from my own direct experience, I will make an attempt to point out the experiences that were my own.

Please, don't approach my book with an "open" mind. (An intelligent man once said, an open mind is an empty mind) So, please just read it as though you would read any science fiction novel, and after you are through, pick out some of the less bizarre data and kick it around in your head for a few days and see if any of it makes sense to you too.

Who knows, you might end up sitting on the edge of your bed at three in the morning looking for answers to your questions also.

A very intelligent man I came across in my journey to the "LIGHT" once told me, "If it's not true for you, it's not true". So, I don't expect you to take my words for truth.

You will have to experience your own truths on your own journey. I just hope my words will set you on your journey.

I stray off the path a bit in my chapter on world facts, but I enjoyed the stories so much when I received them, I just had to include them in the book.

CHAPTER I Changing Your Personality

Turn the Other Cheek

Have you ever experienced the 'I was only kidding' routine? Let me explain, let's say your spouse, employer, best friend or a member of your family just hit you with an off-the-wall criticism for no reason whatsoever. You make the mistake of lashing back, and for your return lashing you hear, *'what are you getting so bent out of shape about, I was only <u>kidding</u>'.*

When someone does this to you, there is a reason for it that I will try to explain.

Most human beings, (Spirits) need to be <u>right</u> 'all the time'. If someone commits an anti-survival, (overt/covert) act against you, (talks about you behind your back, thinks you are stupid, steals from you, etc. etc.) they have (if they have a conscience) just made themselves wrong. Now, they only have a few methods of bringing themselves back to the 'right' little spirit they 'must' be.

What are those methods?

The first and easiest way is, to get you mad at them by throwing small barbs of criticism, (saying offensive things to you), 'for no reason at all', (things like, 'do you have to wear your hair like that? or Don't you have dinner ready yet, what the ___ have you been doing?'. Once they get you to react angrily, they have justified their previous covert action by proving that you can't hold your temper, you blow up easily or you just can't take a little kidding.

Somehow in their tiny minds, your act of anger at their prodding you is equal to their prior covert act, so now they have reduced you to their level and justified 'in their minds' that you are just as bad as they are, and therefore the 'playing field' is now level again and they feel absolved of all wrong doing.

The more covert acts they commit against you, the longer the game goes on. If you would have applied the teachings of our Lord, Jesus, you would have turned the other cheek, 'not reacted' and you would have stuck this person with their own deeds and no justification for them. If you had turned the other cheek, like saying: (thank you for telling me that), now he/she would have been stuck with their original covert act against you and would have had to live with their 'covert act' or look for another alternative.

By the way, the second alternative possible for the evildoer, (as President Bush would probably call them), is to bite their lip, not say anything to you and just live with their covert act.

The third alternative is, for them to confess their covert act in full and apologize to you for the act. By the way, if someone you know is always using the phrase 'I was only kidding', just explain to them the above reason why they do it, and then the next time they do it to you, just ask them, "ok, what are you doing to me I don't know about". If they have any conscience at all, they will turn pale, right before your eyes.

How pale depends on the severity of the deed. If they won't give up their deed, and if you are still curious about what their deed was, you can throw several outlandish examples at them, such as: did you kill my dog? Did you wreck my car? Did you empty my bank account?

After hearing these outrageous examples, and if you keep it up long enough to break them down, you might possibly get the deed out of them. (I ate the last candy bar out of the cupboard that you said was yours). After learning this little game and how it works, your life will never be the same.

After everyone learns what you now know, the people who steer clear of you, or treat you with kid gloves, are now taking care to keep their rumors about you to themselves, and if they are still committing covert deeds against you, they are now biting their lips, holding in their criticisms and living with the deeds.

(You have just learned how to turn the other cheek).

Interesting/Interested

Getting on to happier subjects, have you ever observed young teens in groups talking with one another? If you know what to look for, it's almost as much fun as watching a good comedy movie.

If one teen is being interesting (showing off), to another, and the other teen is also being interesting (showing off). Their antics can entertain you all day long. The trick they need to learn is, 'when to be interesting' and 'when to be interested'.

One great change you can make to your personality is to become a good listener and to be able to recognize when you should be listening, (being interested) and when you should be talking, (being interesting).

If a boy is standing on his head making loud noises and the girl is fluffing her hair and looking at herself in a mirror, they are both trying to be interesting and the game will go nowhere.

You can change your personality for the better if you only learn this one little trick:
- If the other person seems interested in you, do your best to be interesting.
- If the other person is trying to be interesting, do your best to be interested.

It's that simple. Many people can hardly wait for you to shut up so they can get their two bits worth into the conversation. When people say to you, a penny for your thoughts, don't go on and on putting 'two cents worth' into the conversation. Several times I have said to these people, "do you realize you talk constantly and never give anyone else a chance to speak". I know it's hard to say that to anyone, especially if it's a good friend or if you are one of those people who just can't take the chance of hurting another person's feelings for any reason.

However, think of it this way, maybe you are leading them to a better personality and quite possibly keeping them from driving their friends and loved ones totally out of their minds.

My Father Did It

While I was working at Rockwell International on the Apollo Project, one of the Supervisors I worked with had the bad habit of picking his nose whenever he was in a conversation that put him under pressure. One day several Supervisors and Engineers, including myself were standing around discussing why most of the employees in the Engineering Departments were so depressed most of the time.

As we became more involved and were beginning to assign blame, I noticed that Art, my friend the Supervisor was aggressively picking his nose with his little pinky finger. Being forward and outspoken, I immediately asked him, *"Art, who did you used to know that picked their nose?"* I caught him just right and he answered without even thinking about it. He said. *"My Dad used to pick his nose whenever he scolded me. Why did you ask?"* And as he was talking, he pulled his finger out of his nose, looked long and hard at his finger and said, "Oh my God".

We talked about it for a while and after that, I never saw him pick his nose again. It's in a person's nature to use the personality traits of someone who had control over them for some length of time. I guess the mind determines that if a person wins out over you, you can win out over others by imitating their traits and using them to your own advantage.

So, (for example) if you know someone that has a trait of yelling and shaking their fist to get the upper hand over someone else, they are imitating someone else's prior personality trait that was possibly used against them. If you want to turn the table on them, just start yelling louder and shaking your fist harder at them and you may just emulate the person they are imitating and take them back in time to a place they won't want to go. Many times when you do, they will fold up and turn meek as a lamb.

So, if you are subject to fits of misbehavior, take along look at the people who may have influenced your undesirable personality traits during your upbringing and see if perhaps you aren't mimicking something that was used on you to keep you in line. Don't despair if you don't find anything. This is very heavy duty stuff and not everyone is able to locate sources of bad habits easily.

You have probably heard the saying, *"you tend to hate the things others do that you unknowingly do yourself"*. I have just told you the source of those bad habits.

Having Character

One point I would like to make that might improve your personality is: If you tell someone that you will perform some act or duty in their behalf make sure you follow through and DO IT.

Nothing hurts worse than to have someone promise you that they will be at certain place or do a certain thing for you and then not be there or not do it. I put this under the category of having character or not having character. My Dad used to refer to the latter as 'blowhards'.

Keep your word and keep your reputation clean.

If you have no intention of keeping your word, then don't give it. I have found in my travels, people whose thumbs are extremely pliable and bend backwards very easily have a very hard time saying no. Then they later regret their words and try to find a way out of their promise.

The best solution is to keep the zipper on your lips, zipped closed.

CHAPTER II Making Your Marriage Work

End any Future Conflicts

If you are thinking of, or making plans to get married, before you do it might be a good idea to get some counseling before doing so. Most people spend a lot more time planning their wedding than they do planning their marriage. You might at minimum perform my little pre-marriage program that I picked up during my never ending journey toward knowledge and awareness.

It goes something like this:

You and your intended each need to get an 8.5" by 11" tablet and a pen.

- You should each make long, separate lists of what a Wife should **be** and what a Husband should **be**.
- Then you both should make long separate lists of what a Wife should **do** and what a Husband should **do.**
- Next you both should make long separate lists of what a Wife should **have** and what a Husband should **have**.

Now each of you should make long and separate lists again, only this time putting the word **not** in front of the words, **be-do**-and **have**. Making the sentences read, what a Wife should **not be**, etc. etc.

Completing all the lists may take several days. The more items you put on the lists for each question the better chance you have of getting all the potential problems out in the open. I would suggest that each person have at least 2 full pages of answers to each question.

After you both have exhausted your thoughts and cannot possibly think of another item to put on any of the lists, trade the lists with each other and read what each other has to say.

After a time of studying each list, you should both sit down and come to a compromise over what each of you are going to be, do and have.

Keep the lists for the entire period of your marriage. You may want to add to them or re-negotiate some of the compromises. You may both change considerably as you grow older, and compromising is one of the ways to handle those changes.

My Wife and I were married for 60 years and the only thing we couldn't reach a compromise on was whether the toilet paper should roll from the back of the roll or from the front of the roll. We have had some really heavy arguments over toilet paper. I really believe we need a national poll on the subject of toilet paper orientation. (We truly had a give and take relationship, I would give and she would take-oops another covert act to clean up.)

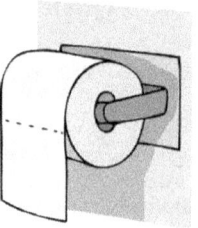

One thing you both should *'have'* with this is FUN.

What! Who Told You That

Another MAJOR thing you can both do to keep your relationship on the straight and narrow is: **'never'** keep secrets from each other unless the secret involves a surprise party or a gift.

There is a condition, where two people are arguing constantly and can't seem to get along no matter how hard 'one' of them may try, and the 'what are you doing to me I don't know about' question bounces off like water off a duck's back.

Then the next thing to look for is: is there a third person or thing involved.

Most always when one spouse seem bent on destroying the relationship and is constantly criticizing, it could very well be because of a third party person instigating the destruction. By instigating, I mean making up and imparting lies against one of the parties and then making sure the second party hears the lies.

In this case, it is extremely difficult to find the reason, because the second party almost always 'buys' into the lies. You may have to seek professional help to discover what or who the third party is.

A very wise man once told me that if you were untrue, (cheating) to your spouse you must follow certain 'guidelines' in order to be forgiven for your transgressions against your spouse.

- First you must write up your transgressions in full and in great detail.
- You must also write down the reasons you feel you should be allowed to come back into the Family.
- After you have everything written down, make a copy for each person of the age of 18 or over in the Family.
- Each person that receives a copy shall read it and decide if you should be allowed back into the family or not.

- If a majority of the Family members decide you may return, then you must convince your spouse to let you come back.
- You must also perform an act far above and beyond for your spouse. Something on the order of a two week vacation in Hawaii.
- Then you must write down a promise to your spouse to never repeat your transgressions for as long as you are man and wife.

Then and only then can you be forgiven.

If you have made a bad choice for a mate, and have chosen a person with a Type 'A' personality, all the above suggestions are null and void. **Sorry☹.**

Unruly Teens

If you would like to see a perfect example of the *"what are you doing to me I don't know about"* cycle, you need to be around a few unruly teenagers.

Many teens are constantly involved in something they shouldn't be involved in. This causes them to very often be very belligerent toward their parents.

Teens that are being ethical and staying out of trouble have no reason to curse and backtalk their parents. If you observe one that does, you can bet, asking them, the: 'what are you doing to me I don't know about question', will bring hellfire and brimstone out of them.

Be prepared to continue the question until you get an answer. Try the "did you steal money from me?", "Did you kill someone?", "Are you taking drugs?", "Etc. Etc." questions and maybe you will get lucky and dig out the truth and set them free and bring yourself some peace and light.

Alarm Clock Trick

My Wife's parents both died in their early years, so my Wife and I brought her fourteen year old Sister home to live with us. My Wife and I being very young ourselves had to 'learn' how to raise a teenager long before we normally would have had to do with our own two young girls.

One of the major situations that ensued was about; what time did you get in last night? I was working as an Engineer at Rockwell during the day and operating our slot car track shop until ten o'clock every night, so I was usually exhausted and went to bed ASAP.

We had very strict rules for my Wife's Sister and were adamant about her curfew time. My Mother had given her a car when she got her driver's license and she loved to stay out late-late-late. I hate to say it but, she always lied about what time she came home.

So, I bought a cheap electric alarm clock and plugged it into a wall plug by the front door. Luckily the wall plug was behind the couch and I was able to hide the clock from her view.

The wall plug was controlled by the light switch near the front door, and it also controlled a small lamp that sat next to the couch. I would leave the lamp on for her and when she came home late at night she would turn off the small lamp with the switch by the door and turn off the **clock** at the same time allowing me to look at the clock in the morning and tell her exactly when she came in, right to the minute.

My Wife's Sister was amazed that I was so clairvoyant and this worked well for a long time right up until I made the mistake of bragging about it to my Wife's other Sister and she in turn told on me.

I hope the above suggestions will bring some "LIGHT" into your lives.

CHAPTER III
Little Known World Facts (or Fiction?)

Fact or Fiction

I can't verify which are true and which are not. So, just read them for the entertainment value until someone with a stronger resume' than mine, declares them true or false, (or you experience them for yourself). They are not in any order, or in any categories.

Please consult your Doctor before using any of the medical suggestions written in this book.

Some of the dark and best kept secrets about our Social Security

Many years ago in Seattle, two wonderful neighbors, Elliott and Patty Roosevelt, came to visit a friend's home to swim on a regular basis. They were a great couple, full of laughter and stories, that today the friend continues to marvel at. Both are now deceased, but their stories remain.

During the years of their friendship they had many, many discussions about Elliott's parents (President Franklin D. and Eleanor Roosevelt) and how his father and mother never intended for the Social Security and Welfare programs to turn out the way they are today.

Elliott used to say that if his parents returned to earth and saw what the politicians had done to their programs they would have burned all of them in hell.

Here is a story I received regarding the Social Security Program and I immediately thought of Elliott's comments. I hope you will read this and think about it.

Franklin Roosevelt, a Democrat, introduced the Social Security (FICA) Program.

He promised:
- That participation in the Program would be completely voluntary,
- That the participants would only have to pay 1% of the first $1,400 of their annual incomes into the Program,
- That the money the participants elected to put into the Program would be deductible from their income for tax purposes each year,
- That the money the participants put in, was to go into the independent "Trust Fund" rather than into the General operating fund, and therefore, would only be used to fund the Social Security Retirement Program, and

no other Government program, and, that the annuity payments to the retirees would never be taxed as income.

FICA-Who Did It

Since many of us have paid into FICA for years, (the Social Security Fund) and are now receiving a Social Security Check every month and then finding that we are getting taxed on 85% of the money we paid to the Federal Government to "put away" for us – you may be interested in the following:

Q: Which Political Party took Social Security from the independent "Trust Fund" and put it into the General fund so that Congress could spend it?
A: It was Lyndon Johnson and the democratically controlled House and Senate.
Q: Which Political Party eliminated the income tax deduction for Social Security (FICA) withholding?
A: The Democratic Party.
Q: Which Political Party started taxing Social Security annuities?
A: The Democratic Party, with Al Gore casting the "tie-breaking" deciding vote, as President of the Senate, while he was Vice President of the USA.
Q: Which Political Party decided to start giving annuity payments to immigrants?

This is my favorite.

A: That's right! Jimmy Carter! And the Democratic Party of course. Immigrants moved into this country, and at age of 65, began to receive Social Security payments. The Democratic Party gave these payments to them even though they never paid a dime into it.

Then after doing all this lying and thieving and violating of the original contract (FICA), the Democrats turned around and now tell you that the Republicans are the ones who want to take your Social Security away from you.

The worst part of it all is that many uninformed citizens believe them.

Everyone REMEMBERS 911, but do you remember 1987?

At a lecture the other day they were playing an old news video of Lt. Col. Oliver North testifying at the Iran-Contra hearings during the Reagan Administration. There was Ollie in front of God and Country getting the third degree, but what he said was stunning! He was being drilled by a senator; "Did you not recently spend close to $60,000 for a home security system?" Ollie replied, "Yes, I did, Sir." The senator continued, trying to get a laugh out of the audience. "Isn't that just a little excessive?" "No, sir," continued Ollie. "No? And why not?" the senator asked. "Because the lives of my family and I were threatened, sir." "Threatened? By whom?" the senator questioned." "By a terrorist, sir" Ollie answered. "Terrorist? What terrorist could possibly scare you that much?" "His name is Osama bin Laden, sir" Ollie replied. (1987)

At this point the senator tried to repeat the name, but couldn't pronounce it, which most people back then probably couldn't. A couple people laughed at the attempt. Then the senator continued. "Why are you so afraid of this man?" the senator asked. "Because, sir, he is the most evil person alive that I know", Ollie answered. "And what do you recommend we do about him?" asked the senator. "Well, sir, if it was up to me, I would recommend that an assassin team be formed to eliminate him and his men from the face of the earth." The senator disagreed with this approach, and that was all that was shown of the clip.

By the way, that senator was AL GORE.

Tower # 1

Here's another little tidbit for your consideration: A terrorist by the name of Mohammad Atta blew up a bus in Israel in 1986. The Israelis captured, tried and imprisoned him. As part of the Oslo agreement with the Palestinians in 1993, Israel had to agree to release so-called 'political prisoners.' However, the Israelis would not release any with blood on their hands.

The American President at the time and his Secretary of State insisted that ALL prisoners be released. Thus, Mohammad Atta was freed and eventually thanked the United States by flying an airplane into Tower number 1 of the World Trade Center. This story was reported by many of the American TV networks at the time the terrorists were first identified. It was censored in the United States from all later reports.

By the way, the President was BILL CLINTON and his Secretary of State was WARREN CHRISTOPHER

"THE ONLY THING NEEDED FOR EVIL TO WIN
IS FOR GOOD MEN TO DO NOTHING"

A WORD TO THE WISE about e-mail petitions

Here is a word for the wise. E-mail **petitions** are NOT acceptable to Congress or any other municipality. To be acceptable, petitions must have a signed signature and full address.

The same thing applies to "prayer chains" so be wary. Almost all e-mails that ask you to add your name and forward on to others are similar to that mass letter of years ago that asked people to send business cards to the little kid in Florida who wanted to break the Guinness Book of records. These petitions may have spy-ware imbedded within them or at the least are used to collect e-mail addresses for their own financial gain. So, please beware.

THIS IS MIND BLOWING - 2 Tough questions

Question number 1: If you knew a woman who was pregnant, who had 8 kids already, three who were deaf, two who were blind, one mentally retarded, and she had syphilis, would you recommend that she have an abortion?

READ THE NEXT QUESTION AND ITS ANSWERS BEFORE LOOKING AT THE ANSWER TO QUESTION NUMBER 1.

Question number 2: It is time to elect a new WORLD leader, and only your vote counts.

Here are the facts about the three candidates who are running for the office. Who would you vote for?

1. Candidate A

Associates with crooked politicians, and consults with an astrologist. He has had two mistresses. He also chain smokes and drinks 8 to 10 martinis a day.

2. Candidate B

He was kicked out of office twice, sleeps until noon, used opium in college and drinks a quart of whiskey every evening.

3. Candidate C

He is a decorated war hero. He's a vegetarian, doesn't smoke, drinks an occasional beer and has never cheated on his Wife.

Which of these candidates would be your choice?
Decide first....no peeking, then scroll down for the answers.

Candidate A is Franklin D. Roosevelt.
Candidate B is Winston Churchill.
Candidate C is Adolph Hitler.

And, by the way, on your answer to the abortion question:

If you said YES, you just killed Beethoven.

Pretty interesting isn't it? I hope it makes you think twice before judging someone in the future.

Wait until you read this next item:

Never be afraid to try something new.

REMEMBER:
- Amateurs –built the ARK.
- Professionals –built the TITANIC.

Can You Believe This

Can you imagine working for a company that has a little more than 500 employees and has the following statistics?

- 29 have been accused of spousal abuse.
- 7 have been arrested for fraud.
- 19 have been accused of writing bad checks.
- 117 have directly or indirectly bankrupted at least 2 businesses.
- 3 have done time for assault.
- 71 cannot get a credit card due to bad credit.
- 14 have been arrested on drug-related charges.
- 8 have been arrested for shoplifting.
- 21 are currently defendants in lawsuits.
- 84 have been arrested for drunk driving in the last year.

Can You Guess which Organization This Is?

Give Up Yet?

It's the 535 members of the United State Congress.

The same group that cranks out hundreds of new laws each year designed to keep the rest of us in "LINE".

THE LAW IS THE LAW!

If the US government determines that it is against the law for the words "under God" to be on our money, then, so be it. And if that same government decides that the "Ten Commandments" are not to be used in or on a government installation, then, so be it. I say "so be it", because I would like to be a law abiding US citizen. I say, "so be it" because I would like to think that smarter people than I are in positions to make good decisions.

I would like to think that those people have the American public's best interests at heart.

BUT DO YOU KNOW WHAT ELSE I WOULD LIKE?

- Since we can't pray to God, can't Trust in God and cannot post His Commandments in Government buildings, I don't believe the Government and its employees should participate in the Easter and Christmas celebrations which honor the God that our government is eliminating from many facets of American life.
- I would like my mail delivered on Christmas, Good Friday, Thanksgiving and Easter. After all, it's just another day.
- I would like the US Supreme Court to be in session on Christmas, Good Friday, Thanksgiving and Easter as well as Sundays. After all, it's just another day.
- I would like the Senate and the House of Representatives to not have to worry about going home for the Christmas break. After all, it's just another day.
- I'm thinking that a lot of my tax payer dollars could be saved, if all government offices and services would work on Christmas, Good Friday and Easter. It shouldn't cost any overtime since those days would be just like any other day of the week to a government that is trying to be "politically correct".
- Better yet, I think that our government should work on Sundays, (initially set aside for worshiping God) because, after all, our government says that it should be just another day.......
- If this idea gets to enough people, maybe our elected officials will stop giving in to the minority opinions and begin, once again, to represent the 'majority' of ALL of the American people.

Please Dear Lord, Give us the help we need to keep YOU in our country....

The purpose of fighting is to win:

There is no possible victory in defense.
- The sword is more important than the shield and skill is more important than either.
- The final weapon is the brain. All else is supplemental."
- Don't pick a fight with an old man. If he's too old to fight, he'll just kill you.
- If you find yourself in a fair fight, your tactics suck.
- I carry a gun, because a cop is too heavy.
- Beware of a man who only has one gun. He probably knows how to use it.

14

The following statements are said to have been made by Ronald Reagan:

Cold War: Here's my strategy on the cold war: We win, they lose.....

- **Terrifying Words:** The most terrifying words in the English language are: I'm from the government and I'm here to help.....

- **Moses:** I have wondered at times about what the Ten Commandments would have looked like if Moses had run them through the U.S. Congress.....

- **The Taxpayer:** That's someone who works for the federal government but doesn't have to take the civil service examination...

- **Eternal Life:** The nearest thing to eternal life we will ever see on this earth is a U.S. government program......

- **Politics:** It has been said that politics is the second oldest profession. I have learned that it bears a striking resemblance to the first......

- **Economy:** Government's view of the economy could be summed up in a few short phrases: If it moves, tax it. If it keeps moving, regulate it. And if it stops moving, subsidize it......

- **Professions:** Politics is not a bad profession. If you succeed there are many rewards, if you disgrace yourself you can always write a book......

- **Arsenals:** No arsenal, or no weapon in the arsenals of the world, is as formidable as the will and moral courage of free men and women.....

- **One Nation:** If we ever forget that we're one nation under God, then we will be a nation gone under.....

This story is worth telling. This story exemplifies gun control as it should be:

This is a story about a shooting in Butte, Montana – November 5, 2006. It is a story about a shotgun toting pre-teen vs. Illegal Alien Home Invaders.

Two illegal aliens, Ralphel Resindez, 23 and Enrico Garza, 26, probably believed they would easily overpower home-alone 11 year old Patricia Harrington after her Father had left their two-story home.

It seems the two crooks never learned two things: they were in Montana and Patricia had been a clay shooting champion since she was nine.

15

Patricia was in her upstairs room when the two men broke through the front door of the house. She quickly ran to her Father's room and grabbed his 12 gauge Mossberg 500 shotgun.

Resindez was the first to get up to the second floor only to be the first to catch a near point blank blast of buckshot from the 11-year-old's knee crouching aim. He suffered fatal wounds to his abdomen and genitals.

When Garza ran to the foot of the stairs, he took a blast to the left shoulder and staggered out into the street where he bled to death before medical help could arrive.

It was found out later that Resindez was armed with a stolen 45 caliber handgun he took from another home invasion robbery. That victim, 50-year-old David Burien, was not so lucky. He died from stab wounds to the chest.

Do you ever wonder why good stuff like this never makes NBC, CBS, PBS, MSNBC, CNN or ABC news? SO DO I.,

Just the same, THAT is gun control.

Thought for The Day

Calling an illegal alien an 'undocumented immigrant' is like calling a drug dealer an 'unlicensed pharmacist'.

THE UNITED STATES ONE DOLLAR BILL

Take out a one dollar bill, and look at it. The one dollar bill you're looking at first came off the presses in 1957 in its present design. This so called 'paper money' is in fact a cotton and linen blend, with red and blue minute silk fibers running through it. It is actually material. We've all washed it without it falling apart. A special blend of ink is used, the contents of the ink we will never know. It is overprinted with symbols and then it is starched to make it water resistant and pressed to give it that nice crisp look.

If you look on the front of the bill, you will see the **United States Treasury Seal.** On the top of the seal you will see the scales for 'a balanced budget'. In the center of the seal, there is a carpenters square, a tool used for an even cut. Underneath the seal is the Key to the United States Treasury. That's all pretty easy to figure out, but what is on the back of that dollar bill is something we should all know.

Turn the bill over and you will see two circles. Both circles, together, comprise the Great Seal of the United States. The First Continental Congress requested that Benjamin Franklin and a group of men come up with a Seal. It took four years to accomplish this task and another two years to get it approved. If you look on the left side, you will see a Pyramid. Notice that the face is lighted, and the western side is dark. This country was just beginning. We had not begun to explore the West or decided what we could do for our Western Civilization.

The Pyramid is uncapped, again signifying that we were not even close to being finished. Inside the capstone you have the all-seeing eye, an ancient symbol for divinity. It was Franklin's belief that one man couldn't do it alone, but a group of men, with the help of God, could do anything.

"IN GOD WE TRUST"

The Latin above the Pyramid, ANNUIT COEPTIS, means, "God has favored our undertaking". The Latin below the Pyramid, NOVUS ORDO SECLORUM, means, "a new order has begun". At the base of the Pyramid is the Roman numeral for 1776. (MDCCLXXVI). If you look at the right-hand circle, and check it carefully, you will learn that it is on every National Cemetery in the United States. It is also on the Parade of Flags Walkway at the Bushnell, Florida  National Cemetery, and is the centerpiece of most heroes' monuments.

 Slightly modified, it is the Seal of the President of the United States, and it is always visible whenever he speaks, yet very few people know what the symbols mean. The Bald Eagle was selected as a symbol for victory for two reasons: First, he is not afraid of a storm; he is strong, and he is smart enough to soar above it. Secondly, he wears no material crown. We had just broken from the King of England. Also, notice the shield is unsupported. This country can now stand on its own. At the top of that shield you have a white bar signifying congress, a unifying factor. We were coming together as one nation.

In the Eagle's beak you will read, "E PLURIBUS UNUM", meaning "one nation from many people". Above the Eagle, you have thirteen stars, representing the thirteen original colonies, and any clouds of misunderstanding rolling away. Again, we were coming together as one. Notice what the Eagle holds in his talons. He holds an olive branch and arrows. This country wants peace, but we will never be afraid to fight to preserve peace. The Eagle always wants to face the olive branch, but in time of war, his gaze turns toward the arrows.

They say that the number 13 is an unlucky number. This is almost a worldwide belief. You will usually never see a room numbered 13, or any hotels or motels with a 13th floor.

But think about this

The Dollar Bill Contains:
- 13 original colonies,
- 13 signers of the Declaration of Independence,
- 13 stripes on our flag,
- 13 steps on the Pyramid,
- 13 letters in the Latin above,
- 13 letters in "E Pluribus Unum",
- 13 stars above the Eagle,
- 13 bars on the shield,
- 13 leaves on the olive branch,
- 13 fruits
- 13 arrows.
- And for minorities, the 13th Amendment.

Most U.S. citizens don't know this, most children don't know this and their History teachers don't teach this.

Jails and Nursing Homes

Here's what we should do:

Let's put all the Seniors in jail and put the criminals in nursing homes.
- Seniors would have access to showers, hobbies and walks.
- They would receive unlimited free prescriptions, dental and medical treatment, wheel chairs, etc.
- They would <u>receive</u> money instead of having to pay it out.
- They would have constant video monitoring, so they would be helped instantly if they fell or needed assistance.
- Their bedding would be washed twice a week and all clothing would be returned to them.
- A guard would check on them every 20 minutes.
- All meals and snacks would be brought to them.
- They would have family visits in a suite built for that purpose.
- They would have access to a library, weight/fitness room, spiritual counseling, a pool and free education.
- They would have free in-house concerts by nationally recognized entertainment artists.
- They would be provided free simple clothing, (ie: shoes, slippers, pajamas and legal aid upon request.
- There would be private, secure rooms provided for all with an outdoor exercise yard complete with gardens.

18

- Each senior would have a P.C., T.V., phone and radio in their room at no cost to them.
- They would be able to receive all their daily phone calls in their rooms.
- There would be a board of directors to hear any complaints and the ACLU would fight for their rights and protection.
- The guards would have a code of conduct to be strictly adhered to, with attorneys available, at no charge to protect the seniors and their families from abuse or neglect.

As for the criminals:

- They would receive cold food.
- They would be left alone and unsupervised. They would receive showers once per week.
- They would live in tiny rooms, (sometimes with two other roommates) for which they would have to pay up to $5,000.00 per month.
- They would have no hope of ever going home again.

Sounds like justice to me.

Shoe Bomber Sentenced

Remember the guy who got on a plane with a bomb built into his shoe and tried to light it?

- Did you know his trial is over?
- Did you know he was sentenced?
- Did you see/hear any of the judge's comments on TV or Radio?
- Didn't think so!!
- Everyone should know what the judge had to say.

Prior to sentencing, the Judge asked the defendant if he had anything to say. His response: After admitting his guilt to the court for the record, Reid also admitted his allegiance to Osama bin Laden, to Islam, and to the religion of Allah, defiantly stating, "I think I will not apologize for my actions", and told the court, "I am at war with your country".

Judge William Young replied, "Mr. Richard C. Reid, harken now to the sentence the Court imposes upon you". On counts 1, 5 and 6 the Court sentences you to life in prison in the custody of the United States Attorney General. On counts 2, 3, 4 and 7, the Court sentences you to 20 years in prison on each count, the sentence on each count to run consecutively. (That's 80 years). On count 8 the Court sentences you to the mandatory 30 years again, to be served consecutively to the 80 years just imposed. The Court imposes upon you for each of the eight counts a fine of $250,000.00 that's an aggregate fine of $2 million. The Court accepts the government's recommendation with respect to restitution and orders restitution in the amount of $298.17 to Andre Bousquet and $5,784.00 to American Airlines.

The Court imposes upon you an $800.00 special assessment. The Court imposes upon you five years supervised release simply because the law requires it. But, the life sentences are real life sentences so I need go no further. This is the sentence that is provided for by our statutes. It is a fair and just sentence. It is a righteous sentence. Now let me explain this to you. We are not afraid of you or any of your terrorist co-conspirators, Mr. Reid. We are Americans. We have been through the fire before. There is too much war talk here and I say that to everyone with the utmost respect. Here in this Court we deal with individuals as individuals and care for individuals as individuals.

As human beings, we reach out for justice. You are not an enemy combatant. You are a terrorist. You are not a soldier in any war. You are a terrorist. To give you that reference, to call you a soldier, gives you far too much stature. Whether the officers of government do it or your attorney does it, or if you think you are a soldier, you are not----, you are a terrorist. And we do not negotiate with terrorists. We do not meet with terrorists. We do not sign documents with terrorists. We hunt them down one by one and bring them to justice. So, war talk is way out of line in this Court. You are a big fellow, but you are not that big. You are no warrior. I've known warriors. You are a terrorist. A species of criminal that is guilty of multiple attempted murders. In a very real sense, State Trooper Santiago had it right when you first were taken off that plane and into custody and you wondered where the press and the TV crews were, and he said: "you're no big deal".

What your able counsel and what the equally able United States attorneys have grappled with and what I have as honestly as I know how tried to grapple with, is why you did something so horrific. What was it that led you here to this courtroom today? I have listened respectfully to what you have to say. And I ask you to search your heart and ask yourself what sort of unfathomable hate led you to do what you are guilty and admit you are guilty of doing? And, I have an answer for you. It may not satisfy you, but as I search this entire record, it comes as close to understanding as I know. It seems to me you hate the one thing that to us is most precious. You hate our freedom. You hate our individual freedom. You hate our individual freedom to live as we choose, to come and go as we choose, to believe or not believe as we individually choose. Here in this society, the very wind carries freedom. It carries it everywhere from sea to shining sea. It is because we prize individual freedom so much that you are here in this beautiful courtroom, so that everyone can see, truly see, that justice is administered fairly, individually, and discretely. It is for freedom's sake that your lawyers are striving so vigorously on your behalf, have filed appeals, will go on in their representation of you before other judges.

We Americans are all about freedom. Because we all know that the way we treat you Mr. Reid, is the measure of our own liberties. Make no mistake though. It is yet true that we will bear any burden; pay any price, to preserve our freedoms. Look around this courtroom. Mark it well. The world is not going to long remember what you or I say here. The day after tomorrow, it will be forgotten, but this, however, will long endure.

Here in this courtroom and courtrooms all across America, the American people will gather to see that justice, individual justice, justice, not war, individual justice is in fact being done. The very President of the United States through his officers will have to come into courtrooms and lay out evidence on which specific matters can be judged and juries of citizens will gather to sit and judge that evidence democratically, to mold and shape and refine our sense of justice. Do you see that flag Mr. Reid? That's the flag of the United States of America. That flag will fly there long after this is all forgotten. That flag stands for freedom. And it always will. Mr. Custody Officer. Stand him down.

So, how much of this Judge's comments did we hear on our TV sets? We need more judges like Judge Young. Everyone should and needs to hear what this fine judge had to say. These were powerful words that strike home.

POLITICAL SCIENCE

DEMOCRAT:
- You have two cows
- Your neighbor has none
- You feel guilty for being successful
- You push for higher taxes so the government can provide cows for everyone.

REPUBLICAN:
- You have two cows
- Your neighbor has none
- So?

SOCIALIST:
- You have two cows
- The government takes one and gives it to your neighbor
- You form a cooperative to tell him how to manage his cow.

COMMUNIST:

- You have two cows
- The government seizes both and provides you with milk
- You wait in line for hours to get it
- It is expensive and sour.

CAPITALISM, AMERICAN STYLE:
- You have two cows
- You sell one, buy a bull, and build a herd of cows.

BUREAUCRACY, CANADIAN STYLE:
- You have two cows
- Under the new farm program the government pays you to shoot one cow, milk the other, and then pour the milk down the drain.

AMERICAN CORPORATION:
- You have two cows
- You sell one, lease it back to yourself and do an IPO on the 2nd cow
- You force the two cows to produce the milk of four cows
- You are surprised when one cow drops dead
- You spin an announcement to the analysts stating you have downsized and are reducing expenses.
- Your stock goes up.

FRENCH CORPORATION:
- You have two cows
- You go on strike because you want three cows
- You go to lunch and drink wine
- Life is good.

JAPANESE CORPORATION:
- You have two cows
- You redesign them so they are one-tenth the size of an ordinary cow and produce twenty times the milk
- They learn to travel on unbelievably crowded trains
- Most are at the top of their class at cow school.

GERMAN CORPORATION:
- You have two cows
- You engineer them so they are all blond, drink lots of beer, give excellent quality milk, and run a hundred miles an hour.
- Unfortunately they also demand 13 weeks of vacation per year.

ITALIAN CORPORATION:
- You have two cows but you don't know where they are

- You break for lunch
- Life is good.

RUSSIAN CORPORATION:
- You have two cows
- You drink some vodka
- You count them and learn you have five cows
- You drink some more vodka
- You count them again and learn you have 42 cows
- The Mafia shows up and takes over however many cows you really have.

TALIBAN CORPORATION:
- You have all the cows in Afghanistan, which are two
- You don't milk them because you cannot touch any creature's private parts
- You get a $40 million grant from the US government to find alternatives to milk production but use the money to buy weapons.

IRAQI CORPORATION:
- You have two cows
- They go into hiding
- They send radio tapes of their mooing.

POLISH CORPORATION:
- You have two bulls
- Employees are regularly maimed and killed attempting to milk them.

BELGIAN CORPORATION:
- You have one cow
- The cow is schizophrenic
- Sometimes the cow thinks she's French, other times she's Flemish
- The Flemish cow won't share with the French cow
- The French cow wants control of the Flemish cow's milk
- The cow asks permission to be cut in half
- The cow dies happy.

FLORIDA CORPORATION:
- You have a black cow and a brown cow
- Everyone votes for the best looking one
- Some people who actually like the brown one best accidentally vote for the black one
- Some people vote for both
- Some people vote for neither
- Some people can't figure out how to vote at all

- Finally, a bunch of guys from out-of-state tell you which one you think is the best looking cow.

CALIFORNIA CORPORATION:
- You have a million cows
- They make real California cheese
- Only five speak English
- Most are illegal.

Australia Says No Again

This is the second time Australia has done this. The Prime Minister surely isn't backing down on her hard line stance and one has to appreciate her belief in the rights of her native countrymen. It is a breath of fresh air to see someone lead. I wish some leaders would step up in Canada and the USA.

The Australian Prime Minister does it again! This Woman should be appointed Queen of the World. Truer words have never been spoken. It took a lot of courage for this woman to speak, what she had to say for the world to hear. The retribution could be phenomenal, but at least she was willing to take a stand on her and Australia's beliefs. THE WHOLE WORLD NEED'S A LEADER LIKE THIS! Muslims who want to live under Islamic Sharia law were told on Wednesday to get out of Australia, as the government targeted radicals in a bid to head off potential terror attacks. Separately, Gillard angered some Australian Muslims on Wednesday by saying she supported spy agencies monitoring the nation's mosques.

Quote: IMMIGRANTS, NOT AUSTRALIANS, MUST ADAPT...Take It Or Leave It. I am tired of this nation worrying about whether we are offending some individual or their culture. Since the terrorist attacks on Bali, we have experienced a surge in patriotism by the majority of Australians. This culture has been developed over two centuries of struggles, trials and victories by millions of men and women who have sought freedom. We speak mainly ENGLISH , not Spanish, Lebanese, Arabic, Chinese, Japanese, Russian, or any other language. Therefore, if you wish to become part of our society learn the language! Most Australians believe in God. This is not some Christian, right wing, political push, but a fact, because Christian men and women, on Christian principles, founded this nation, and this is clearly documented. It is certainly appropriate to display it on the walls of our schools.

24

If God offends you, then I suggest you consider another part of the world as your new home, because God is part of our culture. We will accept your beliefs, and will not question why. All we ask is that you accept ours, and live in harmony and peaceful enjoyment with us. This is OUR COUNTRY, OUR LAND, and OUR LIFESTYLE, and we will allow your every opportunity to enjoy all this. However, once you are done complaining, whining, and griping about Our Flag, Our Pledge, Our Christian beliefs, or Our Way of Life, I highly encourage you take advantage of one other great Australian freedom, THE RIGHT TO LEAVE. If you aren't happy here, then LEAVE. We didn't force you to come here. You asked to be here. So accept the country YOU accepted. End Quote.

Oil, Oil Everywhere

A few months ago there was a news program on oil and one of the Forbes Brothers was the guest. The host said to Forbes, "I am going to ask you a direct question and I would like a direct answer; how much oil does the U.S. have in the ground"? Forbes did not miss a beat, he said, "more than all the Middle East put together". The U.S. Geological Service issued a report in April 2008 that only scientists and oil men knew was coming, but man it was big. It was a revised report, (hadn't been updated since 1995) on how much oil was in the area of the western 2/3 of North Dakota, western South Dakota and the extreme eastern area of Montana. Check this out.

The Bakken is the largest domestic oil discovery since Alaska's Prudhoe Bay and has the potential to eliminate all American dependence on foreign oil. The Energy Information Administration (EIA) estimates it at 503 billion barrels. Even if just 10% of the oil is recoverable-at $107.00 a barrel, were looking at a resource base worth more than $5.3 trillion. "When I first briefed legislators on this, you could practically see their jaws hit the floor. They had no idea", says Terry Johnson, the Montana Legislature's financial analyst.

"This sizable find is now the highest-producing onshore oil field found in the past 56 years," 'The Pittsburgh Post-Gazette'. It is a formation commonly referred to as the 'Bakken'. It stretches from Northern Montana through North Dakota and into Canada. For years, U.S. oil exploration has been considered a dead end. Even the 'Big Oil' companies gave up searching for major wells decades ago. However, a recent technological breakthrough has opened up the Bakken's massive reserves, and now we have access of up to 500 billion barrels. And because this is light, sweet oil, those billions of barrels will cost Americans just $16 PER BARREL. That's enough crude to fully fuel the American economy for 2041 years straight. Now if THAT didn't throw you on the floor, then this next one should – because it's from 2006.

25

U.S. Oil Discovery, the Larges Reserve in the World. Stansberry Report Online: 4/20/2006. Hidden 1,000 feet below the surface of the Rocky Mountains lies the larges untapped oil reserve in the WORLD. It is more than 2 TRILLION barrels. On August 8, 2005 President Bush mandated its extraction. In three and a half years of high oil prices, none has been extracted. With all this mother-load of oil, why are we still fighting over off-shore drilling? They reported this stunning news: We have more oil inside our borders, than all the other proven reserves on earth. Here are the official estimates:

- 8 times as much oil as Saudi Arabia.
- 18 times as much oil as Iraq.
- 21 times as much oil as Kuwait.
- 22 times as much oil as Yemen.

And it's all right here in the Western United States. How can this be? How can we not be extracting this? It's because the environmentalists and others have blocked every effort to help America become independent of foreign oil. Again, we are letting a small group of people dictate our lives and our economy. WHY?

James Bartis, lead researcher with the study says we've got more oil in this very compact area than the entire Middle East, more than 2 TRILLION barrels untapped. That's more than all the proven oil reserves of crude oil in the world today, reports the Denver Post. Do you think 'OPEC' will drop its price, even with this find? You had better think again. It's all about the competitive market-place, it has to be. Do you think 'OPEC' just might be funding the environmentalists?

Do I have your attention yet? Now, while you are thinking about it, do this: tell everyone you meet about this. If you don't take a little time to do this, then you should stifle yourself the next time you complain about gas prices. Call or write your Congressman.

You can check this one on the following link:
http://www.usgs.gov/newsroom/article.asp?

Life Owner Virus

Anyone using internet mail such as Yahoo, Hotmail, AOL and so on. This information just arrived direct from both Microsoft and Norton. You may receive an apparently harmless e-mail titled "here you have it". If you open the file, a message will appear on your screen saying: 'it is too late now; your life is no longer beautiful.

Subsequently you will Lose Everything On Your Computer, and the person who sent it to you will gain access to your name, e-mail and passwords. This is a new virus that started to circulate back in March 2011. AOL has already confirmed the severity of the virus and the anti- virus software's are not capable of destroying it at the time of this writing. The virus was created by a hacker who calls himself 'life owner'. You can confirm this e-mail on Snopes at:
http://www.snopes.com/computer/virus/hereyouhave.asp

HB 1388 has Passed

You just spent $20 million to move members/supporters of Hamas, a terrorist organization, to the United States; housing, food, transportation, the whole enchilada. The 'Drive Bye Media' never mentioned this. Whether you are an Obama fan, or not, everyone in the U.S. needs to know this. H.R. 1388 was passed, behind our backs. It wasn't mentioned on the TV news. It just went by on the ticker tape at the bottom of the CNN screen.

Obama funds $20M in tax dollars to immigrant Hamas Refugees to the USA. This is the news that did not, and will not make the headlines. By executive order, President Barack Obama has ordered the expenditure of $20M in 'migration assistance' to the Palestinian refugees and 'conflict victims' in Gaza. The 'Presidential determination', (isn't that nice?) which allows hundreds of thousands of Palestinians with ties to Hamas to resettle in the United States, was signed and appears in the Federal Register.

Few on Capitol Hill, or in the media, took note that the order provides a free ticket replete with housing, transportation and food allowances to individuals who have displayed their overwhelming support to the Islamic Resistance Movement, (Hamas) in the parliamentary election of January 2006. Now we learn that he is allowing thousands of Palestinian refugees to move to, and live in the U.S. at American taxpayer expense. These important, and insightful issues are being 'lost' in the blinding 'bail-outs' and 'stimulation' packages.

Are you doubtful? To verify this for yourself:
 www.thefederslregister.com/d.p/2009-02-04-E9-2488

Shoplifter in Augusta, Georgia

Orville Smith, a store manager for Best Buy in Augusta, Georgia, told police he observed a male customer later identified as Tyrone Jackson of Augusta, on surveillance cameras putting a laptop computer under his jacket.

When confronted the man became irate, knocked down an employee, drew a knife and ran for the door.

Outside on the sidewalk were four Marines collecting toys for the 'Toys for Tots' program. Smith said the Marines stopped the man, but he stabbed one of the Marines, Cpl. Phillip Duggan, in the back. The injury did not appear to be severe. Afterwards police and an ambulance arrived at the scene and Cpl. Duggan was transported for treatment.

The subject was also transported to the local hospital with two broken arms, a broken ankle, a broken leg, several missing teeth, possible broken ribs, multiple contusions, assorted lacerations, a broken nose and a broken jaw.

These were injuries he sustained when he slipped and fell off of the curb after stabbing the Marine. Now that was a well written Police Report.

Economic Stimulus

Sometime this year, we taxpayers may receive another 'Economic Stimulus Payment'.

This is indeed a very exciting program, and I'll explain it by using a Q & A format:

Q.   What is an 'Economic Stimulus' payment?
A.   It is money that the federal government will send to taxpayers.
Q.   Where will the government get this money?
A.   From taxpayers.
Q.   So, the government is giving me back my own money?
A.   Only a smidgen of it.
Q.   Then what is the purpose of this payment?
A.   The plan is for you to use the money to purchase a high-definition TV set, thus stimulating the economy.
Q.   But isn't that stimulating the economy of China?
A.   Shut Up.

Below is some helpful advice on how to best help the U.S. economy by spending your stimulus check wisely:

- If you spend your money at Wal-Mart, the money will go to China or Sri Lanka.
- If you spend it on gasoline, your money will go to the Arabs.
- If you purchase a computer, your money will go to India, Taiwan or China.

- If you purchase fruit and vegetables, your money will go to Mexico, Honduras and Guatemala.
- If you buy an efficient car, your money will go to Japan or Korea.
- If you purchase useless stuff, your money will go to Taiwan.
- If you pay your credit cards off, or buy stock, your money will go to management bonuses and they will hide it offshore.

Instead, keep the money in America by:

- Spending it at yard sales.
- Go to ball games.
- Spending it on prostitutes
- Spending it on beer.
- Spending it on tattoos.
- (These are the only American businesses still operating in the U.S.)

Conclusion: Go to a ballgame with a tattooed prostitute that you met at a yard sale and drink beer all day.

No need to thank me, I'm just glad I could be of help.

From Anonymous

"When you see that in order to produce, you need to obtain permission from men who produce nothing; when you see that money is flowing to those who deal not in goods, but in favors; when you see that men get rich more easily by graft than by work, and your laws no longer protect you against them, but protect them against you…you may know that your society is doomed".
http://www.youtube.com/watch?v=YLJ2z8BSUPc&feature=related

Did I Understand This Right?

- If you cross the NORTH KOREAN border illegally, you get 12 years of hard labor.
- If you cross the IRANIAN border illegally, you are detained indefinitely.
- If you cross the AFGHANISTAN border illegally, you will be shot.
- If you cross the SAUDI ARABIAN border illegally, you will be jailed.
- If you cross the CHINESE border illegally, you may never be heard from again.
- If you cross the VENEZUELAN border illegally, you will be branded a spy and your fate will be sealed.
- If you cross the CUBAN border illegally, you will be thrown into political prison to rot.

BUT: If you cross the U.S. border illegally, you get:

- A job.
- A driver's license.
- A Social Security Card.
- Welfare.
- Food stamps.
- Credit Cards.
- Subsidized rent or a loan to buy a house.
- Free health care.
- A lobbyist in Washington.
- Billions of dollars, worth of public documents printed in your language,
- The right to carry your countries flag while you protest that you don't get enough respect.

I JUST WANTED TO MAKE SURE I HAD A FIRM GRASP OF THE SITUATION BEFORE WE VOTE ALL THE UNPRINCIPLED IDIOTS OUT OF CONGRESS IN NOVEMBER.

Why Some Men Have A Dog And No Wife:

- The later you are, the more excited your dog is to see you.
- A dog doesn't notice if you call it by another dog's name.
- A dog likes it if you leave a lot of things on the floor.
- A dog's parents never visit.
- A dog agrees that you have to raise your voice to get your point across.
- A dog finds you amusing when you are drunk.
- A dog loves to go hunting and fishing.
- A dog will not wake you up at night to ask, "If I died, would you get another dog"?
- If a dog has babies, you can put an ad in the paper and give them away.
- A dog will let you put a studded collar on it without calling you a pervert.
- If your dog smells another dog on you it won't get mad, it just thinks it's interesting.
- And last but not least: If your dog leaves you, it won't take half your stuff.

To test this theory: Lock your Wife and your dog in the garage for an hour. Then open it and see who is happy to see you!!!

#90 On Your Phone: I received a telephone call last evening from an individual identifying himself as an AT&T Service Technician, (could also be Telus) who said he was conducting a test on the telephone lines. He said that to complete the test, I should push nine (9), zero (0), the pound sign (#), and then hang up. Luckily, I was suspicious and refused.

Upon contacting the telephone company, I was informed that by pushing 90#, you give the requesting individual full access to your telephone line, which enables them to place long distance calls that will be billed to your phone number. I was further informed that this scam has been originating from many local jails/prisons. Do not press 90# for anyone.

Vital Information, don't skip over this one: Here is something your whole family should be aware of: gangs and thieves are now plotting different ways to get a person, (mostly women) to stop their vehicle and get out of their car. Gangs are placing a car seat by the side of the road with a fake baby in it. Then they hide nearby and wait for a woman to stop and check on the abandoned baby.

Note that the location of this car seat is usually beside a wooded or grassy field area and the woman will be dragged into the woods, beaten and raped, and usually left for dead. If it's a man, they are usually beaten and robbed and maybe left for dead too.

IF YOU SEE SOMETHING OUT OF THE ORDINARY LAYING ALONG SIDE THE ROAD, DO NOT STOP FOR ANY REASON!!

DIAL 9-1-1 AND REPORT WHAT YOU SAW. BUT DON'T EVEN SLOW DOWN.

IF YOU ARE DRIVING AT NIGHT AND EGGS ARE THROWN AT YOUR WINDSHIELD, DO NOT STOP TO CHECK THE CAR, DO NOT OPERATE YOUR WINDSHIELD WASHER OR WIPER, BECAUSE EGGS MIXED WITH WATER BECOMES MILKY AND WILL BLOCK YOUR VISION AND MOST PEOPLE WILL BE FORCED TO PULL OVER AND BECOME VICTIMS OF THESE CRIMINALS.

TELL EVERYONE YOU KNOW ABOUT THIS.

This may cause some trouble:

TOP TEN REASONS WHY MEN PREFER GUNS OVER WOMEN:

Ten. You can trade an old 44 for a new 22.
Nine. You can keep one gun at home and have another for when you are on the road.
Eight. If you admire a friend's gun, and tell him so, he will probably let you try it out a few times.
Seven. Your primary gun doesn't mind if you keep another gun for backup.
Six. Your gun will stay with you even if you run out of ammo.
Five. A gun doesn't take up a lot of closet space.

Four. Guns function normally every day of the month.
Three. A gun doesn't ask, "Do these new grips make me look fat"?
Two. A gun doesn't mind if you go to sleep after you use it.

And the number one reason Why Men Prefer Guns Over Women.
One. You can buy a silencer for a gun.

Bye, 'Bye Hershey'

This is a sad story for those of us who remember growing up with Hershey bars, and just as sad for the generations of today. What will be outsourced next? Pennsylvania is a big state, but it amazes me in this day, how some news doesn't make it over the mountain to the front pages of our papers. Milton Hershey, this year, will be joining H.J. Heinz in rolling over in his grave. Hershey chocolate is moving to MEXICO...They are even closing down Hershey Canada. I think I will be boycotting Hershey.

M.S. Hershey had a dream ... I will buy my OWN Sugar, Milk, Cocoa beans, (all natural mind you) and make candy ... (no tariffs, etc.) EVEN during the depression ... He and the Company made money. Now some corporate big wigs are ruining the name ... AND the product M.S. created.

So, Hershey executives are closing plants in the U.S., laying off over a thousand people, and destroying Mr. Hershey's dream, all to cut labor, material costs and to AVOID PAYING ANY U.S. TAXES! The company will save about $170 million a year, all on the backs of the American people. The top executives will still make their mega bucks and the laid off workers will have to find other jobs, some probably at minimum wages due to their age.

We must all band together and let our Politicians in Washington know we are fed up with NAFTA, CAFTA and 'SHAFTA'.

Who's next?... Welch's, Smucker's? I wouldn't bet my job on it....I for one have tasted chocolate bars made in Mexico, and if the Mexican 'Hershey' chocolate bars taste anything like those, I will never buy another Hershey bar again.

A Firearms Refresher Course:

- An armed man is a citizen. An unarmed man is a subject.
- A gun in the hand is better than a cop on the phone.
- Colt: The original point and click interface.
- Gun control is not about guns; it's about control.
- If guns are outlawed, can we use swords?
- If guns cause crime, then pencils must cause misspelled words.
- Free men do not ask permission to bear arms.

- If you don't know your rights, you don't have any.
- Those who trade liberty for security have neither.
- The United States Constitution © 1791. All rights reserved.
- What part of "shall not be infringed" do you not understand?
- The second amendment is in place in case the politicians ignore the others.
- 64,999,987 firearms owners killed no one yesterday.
- Guns only have two enemies, rust and politicians.
- Know guns, know peace and know safety. No guns, no peace and no safety.
- You don't shoot to kill, you shoot to stay alive.
- Dial 911: Government sponsored Dial-a-Prayer.
- Assault is a behavior, not a device.
- Criminals love gun control, it makes their jobs safer.
- If guns cause crime, then matches must cause arson.
- Only a government that is afraid of its citizens tries to control them.
- You only have the rights you are willing to fight for.
- Enforce the gun control laws we ALREADY have, don't make more.
- When you remove the people's right to bear arms, you create slaves.
- The American Revolution would never have happened with gun control.

Some little known American Naval military history

The U.S.S. Constitution (Old Ironsides) as a combat vessel carried 48,600 gallons of fresh water for her crew of 475 officers and men. This was sufficient to last six months of sustained operations at sea. She carried no evaporators.

However, let it be noted that according to her log, "On July 27, 1798, the U.S.S. Constitution sailed from Boston with a full complement of 475 officers and men, 48,600 gallons of fresh water, 7,400 cannon-shot, 1,600 pounds of black powder and 79,400 gallons of rum." Her mission: "To destroy and harass English shipping." Making Jamaica on October 6, she took on 826 pounds of flour and 68,300 gallons of rum. Then she headed for the Azores, arriving there November 12. She provisioned with 550 pounds of beef and 64,300 gallons of Portuguese wine.

On November 18, she set sail for England. In the ensuing days she defeated five British men-of-war and captured and scuttled 12 English merchantmen, salvaging only the rum aboard each.

By January 26, her powder and shot were exhausted. Nevertheless, although unarmed she made a night raid up the Firth of Clyde in Scotland. Her landing party captured a whisky distillery and transferred 40,000 gallons of single malt scotch aboard by dawn. Then she headed home. The U.S.S. Constitution arrived in Boston on February 20, 1799, with no cannon shot, no food, no powder, no rum, no wine, no whiskey and 38,600 gallons of stagnant water.

THE NAVY RULES!

For Those Who Thought They Knew Everything, Here's A Refresher Course:

I'm Nuts for Coconuts: The liquid inside young coconuts can be used as a substitute for Blood Plasma.

7 Times? No piece of paper can be folded in half more than seven (7) times. Oh go ahead. I'll wait

Unbelievable: Donkeys kill more people annually than airplane crashes do.

Little Acorns: Oak trees do not produce acorns until they are fifty (50) years of age or older.

Watch less TV: You burn more calories sleeping than you do watching television.

Bar Codes: The first product to have a bar code was Wrigley's gum.

Clean Shaven: The King of Hearts is the only king without a moustache.

Expensive Olives: American Airlines saved $40,000 in 1987 by eliminating one (1) olive from each salad served in first-class.

How True, How True: Venus is the only planet that rotates clockwise. (Since Venus is normally associated with women, what does this tell you!).

Wake Up: Apples, not caffeine, are more efficient at waking you up in the morning.

Dead Skin: Most dust particles in your house are made from dead skin.

Cigarette Anyone? The first owner of the Marlboro Company died of lung cancer. So did the first "Marlboro Man".

EEK! Walt Disney was afraid of mice.

Who would have thought: Pearls melt in vinegar.

2006 Data: The three most valuable brand names on earth: Marlboro, Coca Cola and Budweiser, in that order.

Holy Cow: It is possible to lead a cow upstairs, but not downstairs.

Quack, Quack: A duck's quack doesn't echo, and no one knows why.

EUU: Dentists have recommended that your toothbrush be kept at least six (6) feet away from a toilet to avoid airborne particles resulting from the flush. (I keep my toothbrush in the living room now).

Criminals: Richard Millhouse Nixon was the first U.S. president whose name contains all the letters from the word "criminal". The second: William Jefferson Clinton. (Please don't tell me you're surprised!).

Breathless: Turtles can breathe through their butts. (I know some politicians like that, don't you?)

Smoked it Too? The Declaration of Independence was written on hemp (marijuana) paper.

Tittleating: The dot over the letter I is called a "tittle".

More Bounce to the Ounce: A raisin dropped into a glass of fresh champagne will bounce up and down continuously from the bottom of the glass to the top.

Wow: Susan Lucci is the daughter of Phyllis Diller.

What! The 'spot' on 7-UP comes from its inventor, who had red eyes. He was an Albino.

I Knew That: Warren Beatty and Shirley McLain are brother and sister.

Sharks: Orcas (killer whales) kill sharks by torpedoing up into the sharks stomach from underneath, causing the shark to explode.

Sounds Fishy to Me: Most lipstick contains fish scales.

None Fit Him: Donald Duck comics were banned from Finland because he doesn't wear pants.

I Rest My Case: Upper and lower case letters are named 'upper' and 'lower' because in the time when all original print had to be set in individual letters, the 'upper case' letters were stored in the case on top of the case that stored the smaller, 'lower case' letters.

Peter Who? The name Wendy was made up for the book Peter Pan; there was never a recorded Wendy before.

Strange: There are no words in the dictionary that rhyme with the words; orange, purple and silver.

Can't wait to try this: A tiny amount of liquor on a scorpion will make it instantly go mad and sting itself to death.

Boo! The mask used by Michael Myers in the original "Halloween" was a Captain Kirk's mask painted white.

So What! If you have three quarters, four dimes and four pennies, you have $1.19. You also have the largest amount of money in coins without being able to make change for a dollar.

Interesting: The first product Motorola started to develop was a record player for automobiles. At that time, the most well-known player on the market was the Victrola, so they called themselves 'Motorola'.

Eat All You Want: Celery has negative calories. It takes more calories to eat a piece of celery than the celery has in it to begin with. It's the same for apples.

Boo Hoo: Chewing gum while peeling onions will keep you from crying.

That Figures: The glue on Israeli postage stamps is certified kosher.

Educated Thieves: The Guinness Book of Records holds the record for being the book most often stolen from Public Libraries.

Pull My Finger-not: Astronauts are not allowed to eat beans before they go into space because passing wind in a space-suit damages it.

Makes Sense to Me: Isn't it crazy-they put Martha Stewart behind bars while O.J. Simpson, Kobe Bryant and Osama Bin Laden were let free. They take the ONE woman in America willing to cook, clean, and work in the yard, and they haul her fanny off to jail.

Didn't Work For Me: If you Peel a banana from the bottom and you won't have to pick off the little "stringy things". That is how the primates do it.

How Do You Hang Them Up Then? Take your bananas apart when you get home from the store. If you leave them connected at the stem, they ripen faster.

Aluminum Foil? Store your opened chunks of cheese in aluminum foil and cheese will stay fresh much longer and not mold.

This is Hot! Peppers with 3 bumps on the bottom are sweeter and better for eating. Peppers with 4 bumps on the bottom are firmer and better for cooking.

This Works: Add a teaspoon of water when frying ground beef. It will help pull the grease away from the meat while cooking.

I Don't Like Sour Crème: To really make scrambled eggs or omelets rich, add a couple of spoonful's of sour cream, cream cheese, or heavy cream in and then beat them together.

What, No Columbian Gold: For a cool brownie treat, make brownies as directed. Melt Andes mints in a double broiler and pour them over the warm brownies. Let it set for a wonderful mint frosting.

Watch Your Breath: Add garlic immediately to a recipe if you want a light taste of garlic or add garlic at the end of the recipe if you want a stronger taste of garlic.

Mmm Gooood: Snickers Bars make a delicious dessert. Simply chop them up with a food chopper. Peel, core and slice a few apples. Place them in a baking dish and sprinkle the chopped candy bars over the apples. Bake at 350 for 15 minutes. Serve by itself or with ice cream.

This Works: Heat up leftover pizza in a nonstick skillet on top of the stove. Set the heat to medium-low and heat until warm. This keeps the crust crispy, unlike soggy microwave pizza.

Works Great: Put hardboiled egg yolks in a zip lock bag. Seal the baggy and mash the yolks until they are all broken up. Add the remainder of the Deviled Egg ingredients reseal and continue mashing until all ingredients are thoroughly mixed together. Cut off one corner tip of the baggy, squeeze the mixture into the egg white halves and you are finished without the usual mess.

Wash Your Filter: To clean the lint filter of your clothes dryer, especially if you use dryer sheets, wash for about one minute in hot soapy water with a small brush or toothbrush every six months. This removes the waxy coating that dryer sheets leave on the filter. You will save money on your utility bill, extend the life of your dryer's heating element and help protect your house from dryer fires.

Here are some statistics that you may find interesting:

Doctors

- The number of doctors in the U.S. is 700,000.
- The number of accidental deaths caused by physicians each year: 120,000.
- The percentage of accidental deaths per physician is 17.14%.
- Statistics courtesy of the U.S. Dept. of Health & Human Services

Guns:

- The number of gun owners in the U.S. is 80,000,000. Yes, that is 80 million.
- The number of accidental gun deaths per year, all age groups, is 1,500.
- The number of accidental deaths per gun owner is 0.001875%
- Statistics courtesy of the FBI.

So, statistically, doctors are approximately 9,000 times more dangerous than gun owners.

Remember guns do not kill people, doctors do.

FACT: NOT EVERYONE HAS A GUN, BUT ALMOST EVERYONE HAS AT LEAST ONE DOCTOR.

Please alert your friends to this alarming threat. We must ban doctors before this gets completely out of hand. Out of concern for the public at large, I have withheld Statistics on lawyers, lest the shock would cause people to panic and seek medical attention.

More data for your think tank:

Rule of Thumb: In the 1400's a law was set forth in England that a man was allowed to beat his Wife with a stick no thicker than his thumb. Hence we have "the rule of thumb".

Golf: Many years ago in Scotland, a new game was invented. It was ruled "Gentlemen Only....Ladies Forbidden" ... and thus the word GOLF entered into the English language.

The Flintstones: The first couple to be shown in bed together on prime time TV was Fred and Wilma Flintstone.

Monopoly: Every day more money is printed for Monopoly than the U.S. Treasury. (2006 data).

Men vs. Women: Men can read smaller print than women can; women hear better.

Coca Cola: Coca Cola was originally green.

Elbows: It is impossible to lick your own elbow. Go ahead, try, I'll wait.

Alaska: The State with the highest percentage of people who walk to work: Alaska.

Wilderness: The percentage of Africa that is wilderness: 28%. (now get this) The percentage of North America that is wilderness: 38%.

Raising a Dog: The average cost of raising a medium-size dog to the age of eleven: is $16,400.

Airborne People: The average number of people airborne over the U.S. in any given hour: 61,000.

Hair: Intelligent people have more zinc and copper in their hair.

Typewriter: The first novel ever written on a typewriter: 'Tom Sawyer'.

Cable Cars: The San Francisco Cable cars are the only mobile National Monuments.

Kings: Each king in a deck of playing cards represents a great king from history:
- Spades: King David.
- Hearts: Charlemagne.
- Clubs: Alexander, the Great.
- Diamonds: Julius Caesar.

Weird Numbers: 111,111,111 times 111,111,111 = 12,345,678,987,654,321.

Statues: If a statue in the park of a person on a horse has both front legs in the air, the person died in battle. If the horse has one front leg in the air, the person died as a result of wounds received in battle. If the horse has all four legs on the ground, the person died of natural causes.

July 4th: Only two people signed the Declaration of Independence on July 4th, John Hancock and Charles Thompson. Most of the rest signed on August 2, but the last signature wasn't added until five years later.

Boat Names: Most boat owners name their boats. This is the most popular name requested: Obsession.

Spelling Numbers: If you were to spell out numbers, how far would you have to go until you would find the letter "A". Answer: One Thousand.

Honey: What is the only food that never ever spoils? It's Honey.

Collect Calls: On which day are there more collect calls than any other day of the year? It's Father's Day.

Sleep Tight: In Shakespeare's time, mattresses were secured on bed frames with ropes. When you pulled on the ropes the mattress tightened, making the bed firmer to sleep on. Hence the phrase: "goodnight, sleep tight."

Honeymoon: It was the accepted practice in Babylon 4,000 years ago that for a month after the wedding, the bride's Father would supply his Son-in-law with all the mead he could drink during the month. Mead is a honey beer and because their calendar was lunar based, this period was called the honey month, which we know today as the Honeymoon.

Pints and Quarts: In English pubs, ale is ordered by pints and quarts...So, in old England when customers got unruly, the bartender would yell at them, "mind your pints and quarts and settle down." It's where we get the phrase, "mind your P's and Q's." This spilled over into the United States and was used during the prohibition days. When Federal agents, (Revenuers) were known to be in the area of the local distilleries, (the moonshine whiskey stills) word went out for all the people involved to watch their P's and Q's. Or in other words pick up your pints and quarts of moonshine and get the heck out of there before the Revenuers catch you.

Slow Poke: Have you ever wondered where the term 'slow poke' originated? Here's one story that I heard. Back in the early days of the California Gold Rush, there were many gold miners panning for gold in the Northern California streams and rivers. Bending over and shaking their gold pans all day long out in the hot sun was not easy work. Many miners went to bed every night with nagging back aches. To alleviate the pain the miners would take breaks during the day and walk up or down the creek or river and check on the other miners to see how they were doing. If they asked a miner how he was doing he would sometimes get the response, "It's a slow poke day". The miners carried their small flakes of gold in a small leather pouch which they hung from their belts. If the pouch was slow in filling that day they called the day a 'slow poke day'.

Wet Your Whistle: Many years ago in England pub frequenters had a whistle baked into the rim, or handle, of their ceramic cups. When they needed a refill, they used the whistle to get some service. "Wet your whistle" is the phrase inspired by this practice.

Cell Phones: There are a few things that can be done in times of grave emergencies. Your mobile phone can actually be a life saver or an emergency tool for your survival. Check out the things you can do with it:

FIRST: In an Emergency: The Emergency Number worldwide for Mobile Phones is 112. If you find yourself out of the coverage area of your mobile network and you have an emergency, dial 112 and the mobile will search any existing network to establish the emergency number for you, and interestingly this number, 112, can be dialed even if the keypad is locked.

SECOND: Does your car have remote keyless entry? This may come in handy someday. Good reason to own a cell phone: If you lock your keys in the car and the spare keys are at home, call someone at home from your cell phone. Hold your cell phone about one foot from your car door and have the person at your home hold the remote near their phone and push the 'unlock' button. Your car should unlock. It saves someone from having to bring you the spare remote or having a locksmith come to 'jimmy' your lock for a fee. Distance is no object. You could be hundreds of miles away, and if you can reach someone who has the other "remote" for your car, you can unlock the doors (or the trunk). Try it out before you put your fate in this e-mail.

THIRD: If your cell battery is very low, you can activate it by pressing the keys ***3370#**. Your phone will restart with this reserve and the phone will show a 50% increase in battery power. This reserve will get re-charged the next time you charge your phone.

FOURTH: To check your Mobile phone's serial number, key in the following digits on your phone: ***#06#A15** and your serial number code will appear on the screen. This number is unique to your phone. Write it down and keep it somewhere safe. If your phone gets stolen, you can phone your service provider and give them the code. They will then be able to block your handset so even if the thief changes the SIM card, your phone will be totally useless. You might not get your phone back, but at least you know that whoever stole it won't be able to use or sell it either. If everybody does this, there would be no point in people stealing mobile phones.

FIFTH: Cell phone companies are charging us for using the 411 information calls when they really don't have to. When you need to use the 411 information option, simply dial **1-800-373-3411** and you will get the 411 services without incurring any charges whatsoever. You can program the number into your cell phone contact list and have it handy at all times.

Things to make you think a little

There were 39 combat related killings in Iraq in the month of January of 2006. In the fair city of Detroit there were 35 murders in the month of January 2006. That's just one American city about as deadly as the entire war-torn country of Iraq.

When some claim that President Bush shouldn't have started this war, tell them the following:

FDR led us into World War II. Germany never attacked us; Japan did. From 1941 through 1945, - 450,000 lives were lost, (An average of 112,000 lives per year.)

Harry Truman finished that war and then started one in Korea. North Korea never attacked us. From 1950 through 1953, - 55,000 lives were lost, (An average of 18,334 lives per year.)

John F. Kennedy started the Vietnam conflict in 1962. Vietnam never attacked us.

Johnson turned Vietnam into a quagmire. From 1965 through 1975, - 58,000 lives were lost, (An average of 5,800 lives per year.)

Bill Clinton went to war in Bosnia without UN or French consent. Bosnia never attacked us. He was offered Osama Bin Laden's head on a platter three times by Sudan and did nothing. Osama has attacked us on multiple occasions.

In the years since terrorists attacked us, President Bush has liberated two countries, crushed the Taliban, crippled Al-Qaida, put nuclear inspectors in Libya, Iran and North Korea without firing a shot, and captured a terrorist who slaughtered 300,000 of his own people. The Democrats are complaining about how long the war is taking. But it took less time to take Iraq than it took Janet Reno to take the Branch Dravidian compound. That was a 51 day operation.

Have you ever wondered which of our Presidents had the lowest IQ

There have been 12 Presidents over the past 50 years, from F.D. Roosevelt to G.W. Bush, who were rated based upon their scholarly achievements. Writings that they produced without aid of staff, their ability to speak with clarity, and several other psychological factors, which were then scored using the Swanson/Crain System of intelligence ranking. The study determined the following IQ's of each President as accurate to within 5 percentage points.

In order of presidential term:

- Franklin Delano Roosevelt (D) 142
- Harry S. Truman (D) 132
- Dwight David Eisenhower (R) 122
- John Fitzgerald Kennedy (D) 174
- Lyndon Baines Johnson (D) 126
- Richard Milhous Nixon (R) 155
- Gerald R. Ford (R) 121
- James Earl Carter (D) 175

- Ronald Wilson Reagan (R) 105
- George Herbert Walker Bush (R) 98
- William Jefferson Clinton (D) 182
- George Walker Bush (R) 91

In order of IQ rating:

- 182 - William Jefferson Clinton (D)
- 175 - James Earl Carter (D)
- 174 - John Fitzgerald Kennedy (D)
- 155 - Richard Milhous Nixon (R)
- 147 - Franklin Delano Roosevelt
- 132 – Harry S. Truman (D)
- 126 – Lyndon Baines Johnson (D)
- 122 – Dwight David Eisenhower (R)
- 121 – Gerald R. Ford (R)
- 105 – Ronald Wilson Reagan (R)
- 098 – George Herbert Walker Bush (R)
- 091 – George Walker Bush (R)

The 6 Republican Presidents of the past 50 years had an average IQ of 115.5, with President Nixon having the highest at 155. President George W Bush rated the lowest of all the Republicans with an IQ of 91.

The 6 Democratic Presidents of the past 50 years had an average IQ of 156, with President Clinton having the highest IQ, at 182. President Lyndon B. Johnson was rated the lowest of all the Democrats with an IQ of 126. No President other than Carter (D) has released his actual IQ (176). Note the institute measured him at 175.

Among comments made concerning the specific testing of President G.W. Bush, his low ratings are due to his apparently difficult command of the English language in public statements, his limited use of vocabulary (6,500 words for Bush vs. an average of 11,000 words for other Presidents), his lack of scholarly achievements other than a basic MBA, and an absence of any body of work which could be studied on an intellectual basis.

The smartest President didn't know enough to keep his pants zipped and the dumbest one thought he could run a war.

Your Government at work:

Once upon a time the government had a vast scrap yard in the middle of the desert.
Congress said, "Someone may steal from it at night."

So they created a night watchman position and hired a person for the job.
Then Congress said, "How does the watchman do his job without instructions?"
So they created a planning department and hired two people, one person to write the instructions, and one person to do the time studies.
Then Congress said, "How will we know the night watchman is doing the tasks correctly?"
So they created a Quality Control department and hired two people. They needed one person to do the studies and one to write the reports.
Then Congress said, "How are these people going to get paid?"
So they created the following positions, a time keeper and a payroll officer and then hired two people to fill the new positions.
Then Congress said, "Who will be accountable for all these people?"
So they created an administrative section and hired three people, an Administrative Officer, Assistant Administrative Officer and a Legal Secretary.
Then Congress said, "We have had this command in operation for one year and we are $18,000 over budget, we must cutback overall cost."

SO THEY FIRED THE NIGHT WATCHMAN!

Try this. It came from an orthopedic surgeon

This will boggle your mind and you will keep trying over and over again to see if you can outsmart your foot, but you can't. It's preprogrammed into your brain.

- Without anyone watching you and while sitting where you are perhaps at your desk in front of your computer, lift your right foot off the floor and make clockwise circles.
- Now while doing this, draw the number '6' in the air with your right hand. Your foot will change direction.

I told you so! And there is nothing you can do about it.

You and I both know how stupid it is, but before the day is done you are going to try it again, if you've not already done so.

I don't know how true this is, but it is interesting

A conversation between a Customer and Bank of America bank;

The Bank: Bank of America, can I help you?
Customer: Yes, I want to cancel my account. I don't want to do business with you any longer.
The Bank: Why?
Customer: Because you are giving credit to illegal immigrants and I don't think it's right. I'm taking my business elsewhere.

The Bank: Well, Mr. Customer, we don't want to see you do that, but we can't stop you. I'll help you close the account. What is your account number?
Customer: (Gives account number).
The Bank: For security purposes and for your protection, can you please give me the last four digits of your social security number?
Customer: No.
The Bank: Mr. Customer, I need to verify your information, but in order to help you, I'll need verification of who you are.
Customer: Why should I give you my social security number? The reason I'm closing my account is that your bank is issuing credit cards to illegal immigrants who don't have social security numbers. You are targeting that audience and want their business. Let's say that I'm an illegal immigrant and you've given me a credit card. I have a question about it and call for assistance. You wouldn't be asking me for a Social Security number, would you?
The Bank: No sir, I wouldn't.
Customer: Why not?
The Bank: Because you would have pressed '2' to speak in Spanish. We don't ask for that information when calling in on the **Spanish speaking only** line.

You can check this out on "snopes" if you like:
http://www.snopes.com/politics/immigration/bankofamerica.asp

I have seen these statistics so many times I don't understand why our Federal and State governments treat it all so lightly:

$11 Billion to $22 Billion is spent on welfare to illegal aliens each year
http://tinyurl.com/zob77

$2.2 Billion dollars a year is spent on food assistance programs such as food stamps, WIC and free school lunches for illegal aliens.
http:/www.cis.org/articles/2004/fiscalexec.html

$2.5 Billion dollars a year is spent on Medicaid for illegal aliens.
http:/www.cis.org/articles/2004/fiscalexec.html

$12 Billion dollars a year is spent on primary and secondary school education for children here illegally and most can't speak a word of English.
http://transcripts.cnn.com/TRANSCRIPTS/0604/01

$17 Billion dollars a year is spent for the education of American-born children of illegal aliens, known as anchor babies.
http://transcripts.cnn.com/TRANSCRIPTS/0604/01/ldt.01.html

$3 Million dollars per DAY is spent to incarcerate illegal aliens.
http://transcripts.cnn.com/TRANSCRIPTS/0604/01/ldt.01.html

44

30% percent of all Federal Prison inmates are illegal aliens.
http://transcripts.cnn.com/TRANSCRIPTS/0604/01/ldt.o1.html

$90 Billion dollars a year is spent on illegal aliens for Welfare and Social Services by the American taxpayers.
http://premium.cnn.com/TRANSCRIPTS/0604/01/ldt.01.html

$200 Billion dollars a year in suppressed American wages are caused by the illegal aliens.
http://transcripts.cnn.com/TRANSCRIPTS/0604/01/ldt.01.html

The National Policy Institute "estimated that the total cost of mass deportation would be between $206 and $230 Billion or an average cost of between $41 and $45 Billion annually over a five year period."
http://www.nationalpolicyinstitute.org/pdf/deportation.pdf

In 2006 illegal aliens sent home $45 Billion in remittances back to their countries of origin.
http://www.rense.com/general75/niht.htm

The dark side of illegal immigration: Nearly One Million Sex Crimes are committed by Illegal Immigrants.

The total cost is a whopping:

$338.3 Billion Dollars A Year.

Oh Well! Ho Hum, I wonder if anyone cares

Here Are A Few More Handy Tips for You---I Haven't Checked Them All---

NO TIME.
Reheating refrigerated bread: To warm biscuits, pancakes or muffins that were refrigerated, place them in a microwave along with a cup of water. The increased moisture will keep the food moist and help it reheat faster.
Broken Glass: To pick up tiny shards of broken glass, dab them with a wet cotton ball. The fibers catch the shards that you can't see.
No More Mosquitoes: Place a dryer sheet (Bounce or?) in your pocket. It will keep the mosquitoes away. I've tried this and it works. I pinned one to my hat.
Squirrel Away: To keep squirrels from eating your plants, sprinkle your plants with cayenne pepper. The cayenne pepper doesn't hurt the plant and the squirrels won't come near it.

Pre-made Thank You notes: When you give a bridal/baby shower, buy a pack of thank you cards for the guest of honor. During the party, pass out the envelopes only and have everyone put their address on one. When the bride/new mother signs the thank you cards she has the envelopes all addressed and ready to mail.

This Bike is Mine: If you purchase a new bike for your child, place their picture inside the handle bar before placing the grips on. If the bike gets stolen and later recovered, remove the grip and there is your proof who owns the bike.

Reducing Static Cling: Pin a small safety pin to the seam of your slip and you will not have a clingy skirt or dress. Same thing works with slacks that cling when wearing panty hose. Place the pin in the seam of slacks and static is gone.

Measuring Cups: Before you pour sticky substances into a measuring cup, fill the cup with hot water. Pour out the hot water, but don't dry the cup. Next, add your sticky ingredient and watch how easily it comes right out of the cup.

Foggy windshield: Hate fogged up windshields? Buy a chalkboard eraser and keep it in the glove box of your car. When the windows fog up, rub it with the eraser. It works better than a cloth or a paper towel.

Reopening Envelopes: If you seal an envelope and then realize you forgot to put something inside, just place the envelope in the freezer for an hour or two. When you take it out, is should unseal easily.

Hair Conditioner: You can use your hair conditioner as a shaving cream to shave your legs. It's a lot cheaper than shaving cream and leaves your legs really smooth. It's also a great way to use up the hair conditioner you bought but didn't like when you used it in your hair. I'm a guy folks, so you girls will have to validate this one for me.

Good Bye Fruit Flies: To get rid of pesky fruit flies, take a small glass, fill it ½ inch full with Apple Cider Vinegar and 2 drops of dishwashing liquid, mix well. You will find those pesky flies drawn to the liquid in the cup and then gone forever.

Goodbye Ants: Put small piles of cornmeal where you see ants. They eat it, take it 'home,' and can't digest it so it kills them. It may take a week or so, especially if it rains, but it works and you don't have the worry about pets or small children being harmed.

Here's another way to end your ant problems. Make a 50-50 mix of 20 Mule Team Borax Soap and regular sugar. To experiment with this, start with just a small amount of each (1 teaspoon each). Mix the two dry ingredients together in a small cup or plastic butter bowl. Drip a couple drops of water into the mix and stir together. Add a drop of water and continue stirring until you get a honey like consistency. Put a small amount on a piece of 2 inch square card paper and then place it on the ant trail. The ants will carry the mixture back to their nest and feed their young and the Queen. No more ants.

A friend of mine had a motel and said this works great and works overnight. Note: This stuff turns hard as concrete overnight so if you get it on or in something you don't want it on or in, clean it up quick before it hardens.

Note 2: Ants kill and eat termites so don't kill all the ants in your yard. Do this overnight and don't let children or pets get into the mix.

Take The Baby Powder to the Beach: Keep a small container of baby powder in your beach bag and when you are ready to leave the beach sprinkle yourself and your kids with the powder and the sand will slide right off your skin.

President Theodore Roosevelt's comments on immigrants: In the first place, we should insist that if the immigrant who comes here in good faith becomes an American and assimilates himself to us, he shall be treated on an exact equality with everyone else, for it is an outrage to discriminate against any such man because of creed, birthplace or origin. But this is predicated upon the person becoming in every facet an American, and nothing but an American. There can be no divided allegiance here. Any man who says he is an American, but something else also, isn't an American at all. We have room for but one flag, the American flag. We have room for but one language here, and that is the English language. We have room for but one sole loyalty and that is a loyalty to the American people.

Here's a Bit More Gun History:

Russia: In 1929, the Soviet Union established gun control. From 1929 to 1953, about 20 million dissidents, unable to defend themselves, were rounded up and exterminated.

Turkey: In 1911, Turkey established gun control. From 1915 to 1917, 1.5 Million Armenians, unable to defend themselves, were rounded up and exterminated.

Germany: Germany established gun control in 1938 and from 1939 to 1945, a total of 13 million Jews and others who were unable to defend themselves were rounded up and exterminated.

China: China established gun control in 1935. From 1948 to 1952, 20 million political dissidents unable to defend themselves, were rounded up and exterminated.

Guatemala: Guatemala established gun control in 1964. From 1964 to 1981, 100,000 Mayan Indians unable to defend themselves, were rounded up and exterminated.

Uganda: Uganda established gun control in 1970. From 1971 to 1979, 300,000 Christians, unable to defend themselves were rounded up and exterminated.

Cambodia: Cambodia established gun control in 1956. From 1975 to 1977, one million 'educated' people, unable to defend themselves, were rounded up and exterminated.

Defenseless people rounded up and exterminated in the 20th century because of gun control, fifty six (56) million.

Australia: It has been 12 months since gun owners in Australia were forced by a new law to surrender 640,381 personal firearms to be destroyed by their own government, a program costing Australian taxpayers more than $500 million dollars. The first year results are now in: Australia-wide, homicides are up 3.2 percent. Australia-wide assaults are up 8.6 percent. Australia-wide, armed robberies are up 44 percent. In the state of Victoria alone, homicides with firearms are now up 300 percent. Note that while the law-abiding citizens turned their guns in, the criminals did not. While figures over the previous 25 years showed a steady decrease in armed robbery with firearms, this has changed drastically upward in the past 12 months, since criminals are now guaranteed that their prey is unarmed. There has also been a dramatic increase in break-ins and assaults of the ELDERLY. Australian politicians are at a loss to explain why public safety has decreased, after such a monumental effort and expense was expended to rid their country of firearms.

You won't see all of this data on the American evening news or hear our president, governors or other politicians disseminating this information. Guns in the hands of honest citizens save lives and property and, yes, gun control laws only affect the law abiding citizens. With guns, we are 'citizens'. Without them, we are 'subjects'.

Signs of The Times: Most retailers have cash registers wherein the clerk posts the amount given and it automatically gives the correct change. Years ago, when I presented cash as shown below, they would sometimes tell me I gave them too much money.

1958-2008: Fifty years of math:

Last week I purchased a burger at Burger King for $1.58. The counter girl took my $2.00 and I pulled 8 cents from my pocket and gave it to her. She stood there, holding the nickel and 3 pennies, while looking at the screen on her register. I sensed her discomfort and tried to tell her to just give me 2 quarters, but she hailed the manager for help. While he tried to explain the transaction to her, she stood there and cried.

Why do I tell you this?

Because of the evolution in teaching math since the 1950s:

Teaching Math in the 1950s

- A logger sells a truckload of lumber for $100. His cost of production is 4/5 of the price. What is his profit?

Teaching Math in the 1960s:

- A logger sells a truckload of lumber for $100. His cost of production is 4/5 of the price, or $80. What is his profit?

Teaching Math in the 1970s:

- A logger sells a truckload of lumber for $100. His cost of production is $80. Did he make a profit?

Teaching Math in the 1980s

- A logger sells a truckload of lumber for $100. His cost of production is $80 and his profit is $20.
- Your assignment: Underline the number 20.

Teaching Math in the 1990s

- A logger cuts down a beautiful forest because he is selfish and inconsiderate and cares nothing for the habitat of animals or the preservation of our woodlands.
- What do you think of this way of making a living? Topic for the class participation after answering the question:
- How did the birds and squirrels feel as the loggers cut down their homes?
               (There are no wrong answers).

Teaching Math in 2008
- Un hachero vende una carretada de maderapara $100. El costo de la producciones es $80.
- Cuanto dinero ha hecho?

Who Said This: "It appears we have appointed our worst generals to command our forces, and our most gifted and brilliant people to edit newspapers! In fact, I discovered by reading newspapers that these editor/geniuses plainly saw all my strategic defects right from the start, yet failed to inform me until it was too late."

"Accordingly, I am readily willing to yield my command to these obviously superior intellects, and I will in turn, do my best for the Cause by writing editorials – after the fact."

Robert E. Lee, 1863

How Big Is Wal-Mart? These are mind boggling statistics on Wal-Mart:

- At Wal-Mart, Americans spend $36,000,000.00 every hour of every day.
- This works out to $20,928 every minute.
- Wal-Mart will sell more from January 1 to St. Patrick's Day (March 17th) than Target sells all year.
- Wal-Mart is larger than Home Depot, Kroger, Target, Sears, Costco and K-Mart all combined.
- Wal-Mart employs 1.6 million employees and is the largest private employer.
- Wal-Mart holds the honor of being the largest company in the history of the World.
- Wal-Mart now sells more food than Kroger and Safeway combined, and keep this in mind, they
- did this in only 15 years.
- During this same 15 year period, 31 Supermarket chains sought bankruptcy, (including Winn Dixie).
- Wal-Mart now sells more food than any other store in the World.
- Wal-Mart has approximately 3,900 stores in the USA of which 1,906 are Super Centers; this is 1,000 more than it had 5 years ago.
- This year, 7.2 billion different sales purchases will be made at a Wal-Mart store. (Earth's population is approximately 6.5 billion).
- 90% of all Americans live within 15 miles of a Wal-Mart store.

Some Might Say This Is Harsh, But It Is The Law:

- There will be NO special bilingual programs in the schools, NO special ballots for elections, and all government business will be conducted in our countries language.
- Foreigners will NOT have the right to vote, no matter how long they are here.
- Foreigners will NEVER be able to hold political office.
- Foreigners will NOT be a burden to the taxpayers. No welfare, NO food stamps, NO health care nor any other government assistance programs.
- Foreigners can invest in this country, but it must be an amount equal to 40,000 times the daily minimum wage.
- If foreigners do come and want to buy land that will be okay, BUT options will be restricted. They are NOT allowed to own waterfront

property. That property is reserved for citizens naturally born in this country.

- Foreigners may NOT protest; No demonstrations, NO waving a foreign flag, NO political organizing, NO 'bad-mouthing' our president or his policies. If you do you will be deported back to your own country.
- If you come to our country illegally, you will be hunted down and sent straight to jail.

The above laws are part of the immigration laws of MEXICO.

How Enron Worked Our President: This is an interesting bit of information that you will not see on any TV reports.

- Enron's chairman did meet with the president and the vice president in the Oval Office.
- Enron gave $420,000 to the president's party over a three year period.
- Enron donated $100,000 to the president's inauguration festivities.
- The Enron chairman stayed at the White House 11 times.
- The Corporation had access to the administration at its highest level and even enlisted the Commerce and State Departments to grease deals for it.
- The taxpayer-supported Export-Import Bank subsidized Enron for more than $600 million in just one transaction.
- But wait—the president under whom all this happened wasn't 'George W. Bush'.

IT WAS PRESIDENT **BILL CLINTON III**

Interesting concept

Tokyo Rose; She had the best music on her station and most GI's just laughed at her. Tokyo Rose broadcasted during World War Two. The Japanese developed a way to demoralize the American forces. Psychological warfare experts developed a message they felt would work. They gave the script to their famous broadcaster "Tokyo Rose" and every day she would broadcast this same message packaged in different ways, hoping it would have a negative impact on American GI's morale.

What was that demoralizing message? It had three main points:

1. Your President is lying to you.
2. This war is illegal.
3. You cannot win this war.

Does this sound familiar?

If it does, is it because Hillary, Harry, John, Teddy and Nancy have all picked up the same message and are broadcasting it on Tokyo CNN, Tokyo ABC, Tokyo CBS and Tokyo NBC to our troops?

The only difference is they claim to support our troops before they demoralize them.

Wait: Come to think of it, every day Tokyo Rose told the troops she was on their side, too!

This History Is Amazing

In 1923 a very important meeting was held at the Edgewater Beach Hotel in Chicago. Attending this meeting were nine of the world's most successful financiers.

Those present were:
- The president of the largest independent steel company;
- The president of the largest utility company;
- The president of the largest gas company;
- The greatest wheat speculator;
- The president of the New York Stock Exchange;
- A member of the president's cabinet;
- The greatest 'bear' in Wall Street;
- Head of the world's greatest monopoly;
- President of the Bank of International Settlements;

Certainly we must admit that here were gathered a group of the world's most successful men. At least, they were men who had found the secret of "making money".

Twenty five years later let's see where these men are:

- The president of the largest independent steel company—Charles Schwab—died bankrupt and lived on borrowed money for five years before his death.
- The president of the greatest utility company—Samuel Insull—died a fugitive from justice and penniless in a foreign land.
- The president of the largest gas company—Howard Hopson—is now insane.
- The greatest wheat speculator—Arthur Cotton—died abroad-insolvent.
- The president of the New York Stock Exchange—Richard Whitney—was recently released from Sing Sing Penitentiary.
- The member of the President's cabinet—Albert Fall—was pardoned from prison so he could die at home.

- The greatest "bear" in Wall Street—Jesse Livermore—committed suicide.
- The head of the great monopoly—Ivar Krueger—committed suicide.
- The president of the Bank of International Settlement—Leon Fraser—committed suicide.

All of these men learned well the art of making money, but not one of them learned how to live happily and to maintain their good fortune.

Happiness is contentment. May you find it and keep it always. A great man I met a few years ago said happiness is having a goal and seeing that you are reaching it. I had my own electronic assembly board house for 32 years and the last 22 years I was working myself to death and not realizing why. The reason is you see, I set a goal to have a company that would provide me with enough money to keep myself and my family financially well and allow me to have all the big boy's toys that I wanted. I reached the goal in about 9 years and from that time on I was working very hard and no longer had a reason for doing so.

You should keep track of yours goals and when you complete them, start new goals to take their place or you will find yourself getting very tired of working.

This is interesting

Please pause for a moment, reflect back, while taking the following multiple choice test. The events are actual events from history. They actually happened. Do you remember?

1968 Bobby Kennedy was shot and killed by:
a. Superman
b. Jay Leno
c. Harry Potter
d. A Muslim male extremist between the ages of 17 and 40

In 1972 at the Munich Olympics, athletes were kidnapped and massacred by:
a. Olga Corbett
b. Sitting Bull
c. Arnold Schwarzenegger
d. Muslim male extremists mostly between the ages of 17 and 40.

In 1979, the US embassy in Iran was taken over by:
a. Lost Norwegians
b. Elvis
c. A tour bus full of 80-year-old women
d. Muslim male extremists mostly between the ages of 17 and 40

During the 1980's a number of Americans were kidnapped in Lebanon by:
a. John Dillinger
b. The King of Sweden
c. The Boy Scouts
d. Muslim male extremists mostly between the ages of 17 and 40

In 1983, the US Marine barracks in Beirut was blown up by:
a. A pizza delivery boy
b. Pee Wee Herman
c. Geraldo Rivera
d. Muslim male extremists mostly between the ages of 17 and 40

In 1985 the cruise ship Achille Lauro was hijacked and a 70 year old American passenger was murdered and thrown overboard in his wheelchair by:
a. The Smurfs
b. Davey Jones
c. The Little Mermaid
d. Muslim male extremists mostly between the ages of 17 and 40

In 1985 TWA flight 847 was hijacked in Athens and a US Navy diver trying to rescue passengers was murdered by:
a. Captain Kidd
b. Charles Lindberg
c. Mother Teresa
d. Muslim male extremists mostly between the ages of 17 and 40

In 1988 Pan Am Flight 103 was bombed by:
a. Scooby Doo
b. The Tooth Fairy
c. The Sundance Kid
d. Muslim male extremists mostly between the ages of 17 and 40

In 1993 the World Trade Center was bombed for the first time by:
a. Richard Simmons
b. Grandma Moses
c. Michael Jordan
d. Muslim male extremists mostly between the ages of 17 and 40

In 1998 the US Embassies in Kenya and Tanzania were bombed by:
a. Mr. Rogers
b. Hillary Clinton
c. The World Wrestling Federation
d. Muslim male extremists mostly between the ages of 17 and 40

On 9/11/2001 four airliners were hijacked; two were used as missiles to take out the World Trade Centers and of the remaining two, one crashed into the US

Pentagon and the other was diverted and crashed by the passengers. Thousands were killed by:
a. Bugs Bunny, Wiley E. Coyote, Daffy Duck and Elmer Fudd
b. The Supreme Court of Florida
c. Mr. Bean
d. Muslim male extremists mostly between the ages of 17 and 40

In 2002 the United States fought a war in Afghanistan against:
a. Enron
b. The Lutheran Church
c. The NFL
d. Muslim male extremists mostly between the ages of 17 and 40

In 2002 reporter Daniel Pearl was kidnapped and murdered By:
a. Bonnie and Clyde
b. Captain Kangaroo
c. Billy Graham
d. Muslim male extremists mostly between the ages of 17 and 40

Nope, I really don't see a pattern here to justify profiling, do you? So, to ensure we Americans never offend anyone, particularly fanatic's intent on killing us, airport security screeners will no longer be allowed to profile certain people. They must conduct random searches of 80 year old women, little kids, airline pilots with proper identification, secret agents who are members of the President's security detail, 85 year old Congressmen with metal hip joints, and Medal of Honor winning and former Governor Joe Foss, but leave Muslin Males mostly between the ages of 17 and 40 alone lest our Country be guilty of profiling.

Let's hope dunder-headed attorneys along with Federal Justices that want to thwart common sense read this and feel doubly ashamed of themselves if they possess any such sense. You folks know who you are!

A Little Brown Bottle of Peroxide: This came over the internet with the story that it had been written by a Doctor's Wife. I am the World's biggest skeptic when it comes to claims about stuff on the internet. I'm putting this in because I have tried 'food grade' peroxide in my spa and it works better than chlorine and doesn't smell as bad. The story goes:

Peroxide was invented during WWI in the 1920's. It was used to cleanse the wounds of our troops and as an antiseptic in our troop hospitals. I submit the following for your pleasure.

- Take one capful and hold it in your mouth for a few minutes every morning, then spit it out. You will have no more canker sores, and your teeth will be whiter without expensive pastes. Use it instead of mouthwashes.

- Let your toothbrushes soak in a cup of peroxide to keep them free of germs.

- Clean your counters and table tops with peroxide to kill germs and leave a fresh smell. Simply put a little on your dishrag when you wipe, or spray it on the counter.

- After rinsing off your wooden cutting board, pour peroxide onto it to kill salmonella and other bacteria.

- I had fungus on my feet for years until I sprayed a 50/50 mixture of peroxide and water on them every night and let them dry.

- Soak any infections or cuts in 3% peroxide for five to ten minutes several times a day. Some people say they have seen gangrene that would not heal with any other medicine but was healed by soaking in peroxide.

- Fill a spray bottle with a 50/50 mixture of peroxide and water and keep it in every bathroom to disinfect without harming your septic system as bleach or most other disinfectants will.

- Tilt your head back and spray into your nostrils with your 50/50 mixture whenever you have a cold or plugged sinus. It will bubble and help to kill the bacteria there. Hold for a few moments and then blow your nose into a tissue.

- If you have a terrible toothache and cannot get to a dentist right away, put a capful of 3% peroxide into your mouth and hold it for about ten minutes several time per day. The pain should lessen greatly.

- Put half a bottle of peroxide in your bath water to help rid boils, fungus or other skin infections.

- Use peroxide to clean your mirrors. There is no smearing.

Note: *Chlorine is a gas and has to be trapped in a solid to allow easy use in your pool and spa. The problem is, the chlorine is usually trapped in saline, (salt). The salt is what burns your eyes and destroys your lawn and foliage. Food grade peroxide comes in liquid form and won't burn your eyes or ruin your vegetation.*

Here's Some Data You Won't Want To Miss: This made me queasy.

- The Garden of Eden was in Iraq
- Mesopotamia, which is now Iraq, was the cradle of civilization.
- Noah built the Ark in Iraq.
- The Tower of Babel was in Iraq.
- Abraham was from Ur, which is in Southern Iraq.
- Issac's Wife Rebekah is from Nahor, which is in Iraq.
- Jacob met Rachel in Iraq.
- Jonah preached in Nineveh, which is in Iraq.
- Assyria, which is in Iraq, conquered the ten tribes of Israel.
- Amos cried out in Iraq.
- Babylon, which is in Iraq, destroyed Jerusalem.
- Daniel was in the lion's den in Iraq.
- The three Hebrew children were in the fire in Iraq, (Jesus had been in Iraq also as the fourth person in the Fiery Furnace!)
- Belshazzar, the King of Babylon saw the "writing on the wall" in Iraq.
- Nebuchadnezzar, King of Babylon, carried the Jews captive into Iraq.
- Ezekiel preached in Iraq.
- The three Wise Men were from Iraq.
- Peter preached in Iraq.
- The "Empire of Man" described in Revelation is called Babylon, which was a city in Iraq.

And you have probably seen this one: Israel is the nation most often mentioned in the Bible. But do you know which nation is second? It is Iraq. However, that is not the name that is used in the Bible. The names used in the Bible are Babylon, Land of Shinar and Mesopotamia. The word Mesopotamia means between the two rivers, more exactly between the Tigris and Euphrates Rivers.

The name Iraq means country with deep roots. Indeed Iraq is a country with deep roots and is a very significant country in the Bible. No other nation, except Israel, has more history and prophecy associated with it than Iraq. And also, this is something to think about: Since America is typically represented by an Eagle; Osama Bin Ladin should have read up on his Muslim passages.

The following verse is from the Koran, (the Islamic Bible)

Koran (9:11) – For it is written that a son of Arabia would awaken a fearsome Eagle. The wrath of the Eagle would be felt throughout the lands of Allah and lo, while some of the people trembled in despair still more rejoiced: for the wrath of the Eagle cleansed the lands of Allah; and then there was peace.

I have seen a couple different versions of this paragraph and have not had time to check the accuracy of the story. Ed.

No, I Am Not Going 'Bananas', but Read This with Trepidation

I don't know how factual this is but I had to include it for its interest factor.

Bananas: Bananas contain three natural sugars – sucrose, fructose and glucose combined with fiber. A banana gives an instant sustained and substantial boost of energy. Research has proven that just two bananas provide enough energy for a strenuous 90 minute workout. No wonder the banana is the number one fruit with the world's leading athletes. But, energy isn't the only way a banana can help us keep fit. It can also help overcome or prevent a substantial number of illnesses and conditions, making it a must to add to our daily diet. (Sounds like a Chiquita add doesn't it?).Oh well – here it is:

Depression: According to a recent survey undertaken by MIND amongst people suffering from depression, many felt much better after eating a banana. This is supposedly because bananas contain tryptophan, a type of protein that the body converts into serotonin, known to make you relax, improve your mood and generally make you feel better.

PMS: Forget the pills – eat a banana. The vitamin B6 it contains regulates the blood glucose levels, which can affect your mood.

Anemia: High in iron, bananas can stimulate the production of hemoglobin in the blood and so helps in cases of anemia.

Blood Pressure: This unique tropical fruit is extremely high in potassium yet low in salt, making it the perfect way to beat high blood pressure. So much so, the US Food and Drug Administration has just allowed the banana industry to make official claims for the fruit's ability to reduce the risk of high blood pressure and stroke.

Brain Power: 200 students at a Twickenham, (Middlesex England) school were helped with their exams this year by eating bananas at breakfast, break and at lunch in a bid to boost their brain power. Research has shown that the potassium-packed fruit can assist learning by making pupils more alert.

Constipation: High in fiber, including bananas in the diet can help restore normal bowel action, helping to overcome the problem without resorting to laxatives.

Hangovers: One of the quickest ways of curing a hangover is to make a banana milk shake, sweetened with honey. The banana calms the stomach and, with the help of the honey, builds up depleted blood sugar levels, while the milk soothes and re-hydrates your system.

Heartburn: Bananas have a natural antacid effect in the body, so if you suffer from heartburn, try eating a banana for soothing relief.

Morning Sickness: Snacking on bananas between meals helps to keep blood sugar levels up and avoid morning sickness.

Mosquito bites: Before reaching for the insect bite cream, try rubbing the affected area with the inside of a banana skin. Many people find it amazingly successful at reducing swelling and irritation.

Nerves: Bananas are high in B vitamins that help calm the nervous system.

Overweight: Studies at the Institute of Psychology in Austria found pressure at work leads to gorging on comfort food like chocolate and chips. Looking at 5,000 hospital patients, researchers found the most obese were more likely to be in high-pressure jobs.
The report concluded that, to avoid panic-induced food cravings, we need to control our blood sugar levels by snacking on high carbohydrate foods every two hours to keep sugar levels steady.

Ulcers: The banana is used as the dietary food against intestinal disorders because of its soft texture and smoothness. It is the only raw fruit that can be eaten without distress in over-chronicler cases. It also neutralizes over-acidity and reduces irritation by coating the lining of the stomach.

Temperature Control: Many other cultures see bananas as a "cooling" fruit that can lower both the physical and emotional temperature of expectant mothers. In Thailand, for example, pregnant women eat bananas to ensure their baby is born with a cool temperature.

Seasonal Affective Disorder (SAD): Bananas can help SAD sufferers because they contain the natural mood enhancer tryptophan.

Smoking: Bananas can also help people trying to give up smoking. The B6 and B12 they contain, as well as the potassium and magnesium found in them, help the body recover from the effects of nicotine withdrawal.

Stress: Potassium is a vital mineral which helps normalize the heartbeat, sends oxygen to the brain and regulates your body's water balance. When we are stressed, our metabolic rate rises, thereby reducing our potassium levels. These can be rebalanced with the help of a high-potassium banana snack.

Strokes: According to research in "The New England Journal of Medicine", eating bananas as part of a regular diet can cut the risk of death from strokes by as much as 40%.

So, a banana really is a natural remedy for many ills. When you compare the banana to an apple, it has four times the protein, twice the carbohydrates, three times the phosphorus, five times as much of vitamin A and iron, and twice the other vitamins and minerals. It is also rich in potassium and is one of the best value foods around. So, maybe its time to change that well-known phrase so that we say, "A banana a day keeps the doctor away!"

Footnote:

If your roses are covered with Aphids, drape banana skins over the branches, it's amazing, but in a day or less, the Aphids are GONE! I personally haven't tried it but what have you got to lose? Give it a shot.

The Clear Button: When I go to pump gasoline into my vehicles from now on, I will be Pushing the clear button before swiping my debit card and after I finish pumping my gas and getting my receipt. If the station employs an un-ethical attendant, he or she can fill their own vehicles from your card if you just walk away from the pump after filling your tank. This may not work with all station pumps, but why take the chance. I know for a fact, in the old days I could fill my car, place the pump handle back into the cradle shutting off the machine, take it out again and then pump gas into my lawn mower gas can without any problem. For myself, I will be pushing the clear button from now on. Push it before you start your transaction and after you get your receipt. I think this only pertains to the older type pumps.

Wow-1850

Do you know what it was like in California back then?
- California became a state.
- The state had no electricity.
- The state had no money.
- Almost everyone spoke Spanish.
- There were gunfights in the street everywhere.

So, basically, it was just like California is today, except the women had real boobs and the men didn't hold hands.

What Is Normal?

It doesn't hurt to take a hard look at yourself from time to time, and this should help get you started:

During a visit to the mental asylum, a visitor asked the Director what the criteria was which defined whether or not a patient should be institutionalized. "Well", said the Director, "we fill up a bathtub, then we offer a teaspoon, a teacup and a bucket to the patient and ask him or her to empty the bathtub." "Oh, I understand," said the visitor. "A normal person would choose the bucket because it's larger than the spoon or the teacup". "No," said the

Director. "A normal person would pull the plug. Do you want a bed near the window?"

Thought you might appreciate the significance of this comparison:

Ed McMahon died not too long ago. He was a great entertainer, but prior to his radio and TV accomplishments he was a Marine Corps pilot in WWII and Korea, earning six Air Medals and attaining the rank of Colonel. After his Korean service, he was subsequently promoted to the rank of Brigadier General in the California Air National Guard.

Farrah Fawcett died not too long ago after a long career in Hollywood as an actress. After she was diagnosed with cancer, she became an activist for cancer treatment and devoted her last remaining years encouraging people to seek treatment. She documented her plight on film and used it to encourage others to stay positive and upbeat despite their diagnosis and suffering.

Michael Jackson died not too long ago. He was perhaps one of the greatest entertainers of modern time. He will also be remembered for his eccentric lifestyle that included sleeping with a chimpanzee, living in a carnival-like atmosphere at Neverland, his fascination with Peter Pan and his numerous masks and costumes.

Question 1) Which of the above did the House of Representatives declare a moment of silence for? (Hint-It wasn't the first two).

Question 2) Which of the above family received a personal note of condolence from President Obama? (Hint-It wasn't the first two).

Does this send a message regarding the state of our country?

Great Orators of the Democratic Party:

- "One man with courage makes a majority".
- Andrew Jackson.

- "The only thing we have to fear is fear itself".
- Franklin D. Roosevelt.

- "Ask not what your country can do for you; ask what you can do for your country".
- John F. Kennedy *(By the way, this is an exact quote from a speech given by Army General Omar Bradley in 1953, just a few years prior to JFK using it in his inaugural speech. JFK or his speech writers recognized a*

great quote, but none credited Bradley for one of the greatest patriotic quotes of all time. Plagiarism, anyone?)

And For Today's Democrats:

- "It depends what your definition of sex is".
Bill Clinton.

- "That Obama, I would like to cut his NUTS off".
Jesse Jackson.

- "Those rumors are false—I believe in the sanctity of marriage".
John Edwards.

- "I invented the internet".
Al Gore.

- "The next person that tells me I'm not religious, I'm going to shove my rosary beads up their ass".
Joe Biden.

- "America –is no longer, uh, what it—it, uh, could be, uh what it once was...uh, and I say to myself, "uh, I don't want that future, uh, uh for my children".
Barack Obama (without his teleprompter).

- "I have campaigned in all 57 states".
Barack Obama.

- "You don't need God anymore, you have us Democrats".
Nancy Pelosi. (2006)

- "Paying taxes is voluntary".
Sen. Harry Reid.

- "Bill is the greatest Husband and Father I know. No one is more faithful, true and honest than he".
Hillary Clinton. (1998).

- Nancy Pelosi said twice, "If the stimulus (spending) package is not passed quickly, then 500 million people will lose their jobs". Since there are approximately 280-290 million people currently living in the United States, total, I would assume the remainder she is referring to are illegal aliens.

I still can't understand why we can't drill for more of our domestic ENERGY:

This is absolutely the funniest joke ever.....ON US!!!

Let it sink in.

Quietly we go like sheep to the slaughter.

Does anyone out there have any memory of the reason given for the establishment of the DEPARTMENT OF ENERGY .... During the Carter Administration?

Anyone?

Anything?

No?

I didn't think so.

Bottom line: we've spent several hundred billion dollars in support of an agency the reason for which not one person who reads this can remember.

Ready??????

It was very simple, and at the time everybody thought it very appropriate:

The 'Department of Energy' was instituted on 08/04/1977:

TO LESSON OUR DEPENDENCE ON FOREIGN OIL.

Hey, pretty efficient, huh?

And now it's 2014, 37 years later and the BUDGET for this necessary Department is at $24.2 BILLION per year.

It has 16,000 Federal employees and approximately 100,000 contract employees and look at the job it has done.

This is where you slap your forehead and say, "What was I thinking".

And now we are turning over the Banking System, Health Care and the Auto Industry to them?

GOD Help US!!

THIS IS NOT A JOKE – VERY SERIOUS

Pass this one on to everybody you know. Anyone that sees a plastic bottle in their yard would think nothing of picking it up to throw it away. Looks like these things are starting to pop up around the U.S. Check it out at the snopes web site below, it's pretty scary.

Important warning! NOT A JOKE! Pay attention to this.

- A plastic bottle with a cap. (Like a normal water bottle).
- A little Drano.

- A little water.
- A small piece of foil.
- Disturb it by moving it; and BOOM (Less than 30 seconds).
- No fingers left and other serious effects to your face, eyes, etc.

People are finding these bombs in mailboxes and in their yards, just waiting for someone to pick it up intending to put it in the trash. It takes about 30 seconds to blow after you move the thing.

See "SNOPES" below ...It's true.
http://www.snopes.com/crime/warnings/bottlebomb.asp

HELLO!

Certain people are angry that the U.S. may start protecting their borders making it harder to sneak into this country and once here, to stay indefinitely. Let me see if I correctly understand the thinking behind these protests. Let's say I break into your house. Let's say when you discover me in your house, you insist that I leave. But I say, No! I like it here. It's better than my house. I've made all the beds and washed the dishes and did the laundry and swept the floors. I've done all the things you don't like to do. I'm hard working and honest. (Except for when I broke into your house).

According to the protesters: You are required to let me stay in your house. You are required to feed me. You are required to add me to your family's insurance plan. You are required to educate my children. You are required to provide other benefits to me & to my family. (My Husband will do all of your yard work because he is also hard working and honest, except for that breaking in part).

If you try to call the police or force me out, I will call my friends who will picket your house carrying signs that proclaim my right to be there. It's only fair, after all, because you have a nicer house than I do, and I'm just trying to better myself. I'm a hardworking and honest person, except for well, you know, I did break into your house, and what a deal it is for me.

I live in your house, contributing only a fraction of the cost of my keep, and there is nothing you can do about it without being accused of cold, uncaring, selfish, prejudiced and bigoted behavior. Oh yeah, **I DEMAND** that you learn **MY LANGUAGE!!!** So you can communicate with me.

Why can't people see how ridiculous this is? Only in America.

Tibetan Personality Test: You just might get some fun out of this one:

Take your time with this one and you will be amazed. The Dalai Lama suggests you read it to see if it works for you. This is very interesting. Be honest and do not cheat by looking ahead at the answers. The mind is like a parachute, it works best when it is opened. This is fun to do, but you must follow the instructions very closely. Do not cheat.

MAKE A WISH BEFORE BEGINNING THE TEST. Write your wish down so you don't forget it. A warning: Answer the questions as you go along. There are only 4 questions and if you see them all before finishing, you will not have honest results. Go down the page slowly, and read and complete each exercise as you scroll down the page. If you have to, cover the paragraphs below with paper so you can't read ahead.

Don't look ahead. Get a pen and paper to write your answers as you go along. You will need it at the end. This is an honest questionnaire which will tell you a lot about your true self. Give an answer for each item. The first thing that comes to mind is usually your best answer as you go along. Remember no one will see this but you.

- Put the following 5 animals in the order of your preference:
    Cow, Tiger, Sheep, Horse, Pig.
- Write one word that describes each one of the following:
    Dog, Cat, Rat, Coffee, Sea.
- Think of someone who also knows you and is important to you, which you can relate them to the following colors. Do not repeat your answer twice. Name just one person for each color:
    Yellow, Orange, Red, White, Green
- Finally, write down your favorite number and your favorite day of the week:

FINISHED?

Please be sure that your answers are what you **REALLY WANT.** Look at the interpretation below: But before continuing. **REPEAT** your wish.

This will define your priorities in your life.
- Cow signifies CAREER
- Tiger signifies PRIDE
- Sheep signifies LOVE
- Horse signifies FAMILY
- Pig signifies MONEY

- Your description of dog implies your own personality.
- Your description of cat implies the personality of your partner.
- Your description of rat implies the personalities of your enemies.

- Your description of coffee is how you interpret sex.
- Your description of sea implies your own life.

- Yellow: Someone you will never forget.
- Orange: Someone you consider your true friend.
- Red: Someone that you really love.
- White: Your twin soul.
- Green: Someone that you will remember for the rest of your life.

You have to share this message with as many people as your favorite number and your wish will come true on the day that you picked as your favorite day. Never stop believing in the journeys you've yet to take, the people you've yet to meet and the stars you've yet to count.

Bounce, Bounce, Bounce: You won't believe this until you try it: All this time you've been putting Bounce in your dryer, well here are a few more suggestions for its use.

- Lay a sheet near an ant trail and watch them go around it. It also repels mice.
- Spread sheets around foundation areas, or in trailers, or cars that are sitting and it keeps mice and ants from entering your home and vehicles.
- It repels mosquitoes. Tie a sheet of Bounce through a belt loop when outdoors during mosquito season.
- It takes the odor out of books and photo albums that don't get opened too often. I have not tried this yet and am concerned about staining the pages with the Bounce chemicals.
- Wiping your Television or Computer screens with a used sheet of Bounce will eliminate the static electricity and keep dust from returning too quickly.
- To dissolve soap scum from shower doors, clean with a sheet of Bounce.
- To make the air fresh in your home, place an individual sheet of Bounce in a drawer or hang one in a closet.
- To keep odor from your carpet getting into your vacuum cleaner, place a sheet of Bounce in the bag.
- To prevent sewing thread from tangling, pull the thread between the folds of a sheet of BOUNCE before sewing.
- To prevent your suitcase from smelling musty, place an individual sheet of Bounce inside your empty luggage just before storing it.
- To make the air fresh in your car, place a sheet under the front seat.

- To clean baked-on-foods from a cooking pan, put a sheet in the pan and fill with water. Let the pan sit overnight and then sponge clean. The anti-static agent apparently weakens the bond between the food and the pan.
- To eliminate odors in wastebaskets, place a sheet of Bounce at the bottom of the wastebasket.
- To collect cat hair, rub the area with a sheet of Bounce and it will magnetically attract all the loose hairs.
- To eliminate static electricity from Venetian blinds, wipe the blinds with a sheet of Bounce. It will also help prevent dust from returning too soon.
- To wipe up sawdust from drilling or sanding wipe with the area with a sheet of Bounce. It works as well as a commercial tack rag. And it's a lot cheaper.
- To eliminate odors in dirty clothes, place an individual sheet of Bounce in the bottom of your laundry hamper or bag.
- To deodorize shoes or sneakers, place a sheet of Bounce in your shoes or sneakers overnight.
- To keep bees away from you, place a sheet of bounce in your back pocket or shirt pocket.
- Put a sheet of Bounce in your sleeping bag and tent before refolding and storing them. It will keep them smelling fresh for the next time.

WHAT!!!!

- **Only in America**---can a pizza get to your house faster than an ambulance.
- **Only in America**---are there handicap parking spaces in front of an ice skating rink.
- **Only in America**---do drugstores make the sick walk all the way to the back of the store to get their prescriptions while healthy people can buy cigarettes at the front.
- **Only in America**---do people order double cheeseburgers, large fries and a **diet** coke.
- **Only in America**---do banks leave both doors open and then chain the pens to the Counter.
- **Only in America**---do we leave cars worth thousands of dollars in the driveway and put our useless junk in the garage.
- **Only in America**---do we use answering machines to screen calls and then have call waiting so we won't miss a call from someone we didn't want to talk to in the first place.
- **Only in America**---do we put hot dogs in packages of ten and buns in packages of eight.

- **Only in America**---do we use the word 'politics' to describe the process so well: 'Poli' in Latin meaning 'many' and 'tics' meaning 'blood sucking creatures'.
- **Only in America**---do we have drive-up ATM's with Braille lettering

EVER WONDER:

- Why the sun lightens our hair, but darkens our skin?
- Why women can't put on mascara with their mouths closed?
- Why you don't ever see the headlines "Psychic Wins Lottery"?
- Why the word "abbreviated" is so long?
- Why it is doctor's call what they do, "practice"?
- Why it is that to stop Windows, you have to click on "Start"?
- Why Lemon Juice is made with artificial flavor and dishwashing liquid is made with real lemons
- Why the man who invests all your money is called a BROKER?
- Why the time of day with the slowest traffic is called rush hour?
- Why they don't make a mouse-flavored cat food?
- When dog food is labeled "new and improved tasting", who tests it?
- Why Noah didn't swat those two mosquitoes?
- Why they sterilize the needle for lethal injections?
- Why they don't make the whole airplane out of the same material they use to make the indestructible black box?
- Why sheep don't shrink when it rains?
- Why they are called apartments, when they are all stuck together?
- If con is the opposite of pro, is Congress the opposite of progress?
- If flying is so safe, why do they call the airport the terminal?

Is This Stupid or What???

- On a Sears Hairdryer: Do not use while sleeping. (That's the only time I have to work on my hair).
- On a bag of Fritos: You could be a winner! No purchase necessary. Details inside. (this is the shoplifter special?)
- On a bar of Dial soap: "Directions: Use like regular soap." (and that would be how?).
- On some Swanson frozen dinners: "Serving suggestion: Defrost." (but it's just a suggestion).
- On Tesco's Tiramisu dessert (printed on the bottom): "Do not turn upside down". (Oh well, duh, a bit late huh?)
- On Marks & Spencer Bread Pudding: "Product will be hot after heating." (and you thought?)
- On packaging for a Rowenta iron: "Do not iron clothes while on your body." (but wouldn't this save more time?)

- On Boot's Children's Cough Medicine: Do not drive a car or operate heavy machinery after taking this medicine. "(We could do a lot to reduce the rate of construction accidents if we could just get those 5-year olds with head colds off those fork lifts.)
- On Nytol Sleep Aid: "Warning: may cause drowsiness. "(and, I'm taking this because?)
- On most brands of Christmas lights: "For indoor or outdoor use only." (as opposed to what?)
- On a Japanese food processor: "Not to be used for the other use." (now, someone out there, help me on this one. I am a bit curious.)
- On Sunsbury's peanuts: "Warning: contains nuts:" (Talk about a news flash.)
- On an American Airlines packet of nuts: "Instructions: Open packet, eat nuts." (Step 3: maybe, uh...fly Delta?)
- On a child's superman costume: "Wearing of this garment does not enable you to fly."
- (I don't blame the company, I blame the parents for this one.)
- On a Swedish chainsaw: "Do not attempt to stop chain with your hands or genitals."(Was there a lot of this happening somewhere?)

Why Our Businesses Go Overseas???

Suppose that every day ten men go out for beer and the bill for all ten comes to $100.00. If they paid their bill the way we pay for taxes, it would go something like this.
- The first four men, (the poorest) would pay nothing.
- The fifth man would pay $1.00.
- The sixth man would pay $3.00.
- The seventh man would pay $7.00.
- The eighth man would pay $12.00.
- The ninth man would pay $18.00.
- The tenth man, (the richest) would pay $59.00.

So, that's what they decided to do. The ten men drank in the bar every day and seemed quite happy with the arrangement, until one day, the owner threw them a curve. 'Since you are all such good customers,' he said, 'I'm going to reduce the cost of your daily beer by $20.00. Drinks for the ten men now cost just $80.00.

The group still wanted to pay their bill the way we pay our taxes, so the first four men were not affected. They would still drink for free. But, what about the other six men, the paying customers?

How could they divide the $20.00 windfall so that everyone would get his fair share? They realized that $20.00 divided by six equals $3.33. But, if they subtracted that from everyone's share, then the fifth man and the sixth man would each end up being paid to drink his beer. So, the bar owner suggested that it would be fair to reduce each man's share by roughly the same amount and he proceeded to work out the amounts each should pay. And, So:

- The fifth man, like the first four, now paid nothing. (a 100% savings.)
- The sixth man now paid $2.00 instead of $3.00. (a 33% savings.)
- The seventh man now paid $5.00 instead of $7.00. (a 28% savings.)
- The eighth man now paid $9.00 instead of $12.00. (a 25% savings.)
- The ninth man now paid $14.00 instead of $18.00. (a 22% savings.)
- The tenth man now paid $49.00 instead of $59.00. (a 16% savings.)

Each of the six men was better off than before. The first four continued to drink for free. But, once outside the bar, the men began to compare their savings.

- I only got a dollar out of the $20.00 declared the sixth man. He pointed to the tenth man, 'but he got $10.00'.
- 'Yeah that's right' exclaimed the fifth man. 'I only saved a dollar too'. It's unfair that he got ten times more than I did.
- "That's true!" shouted the seventh man. 'Why should he get $10.00 back when I got only $2.00? The wealthy get all the breaks!'
- "Wait a minute," yelled the first four men in unison. "We didn't get anything at all. The system exploits the poor!"
- The nine men surrounded the tenth man and beat him up.

The next night, the tenth man didn't show up for drinks, so the nine sat down and had beers without him. But when it came time to pay the bill, they discovered something important. They didn't have enough money between all of them for even half the bill!

And that, boys and girls, journalists and college professors, is how our tax system works. The people who pay the highest taxes get the most benefit from a tax reduction. Tax them too much, attack them for being wealthy, and they just may not show up anymore. In fact, they might start drinking overseas where the atmosphere is somewhat friendlier.

Here's a Popular Viewpoint-Author unknown:

- 'Press 1 for English' is immediately banned. English is the official language: speak it or wait at the border until you can.
- We will immediately go into a two year isolationist posture to straighten out the countries attitude. No imports, no exports. We will use the 'Wal-Mart policy, If we don't have it, you don't need it'.
- When imports are allowed again, there will be a 100% import tax on them.

- All retired military personnel will be required to man one of our many observation towers on our southern border, (six month tour). They will be under strict orders not to fire on SOUTHBOUND aliens.
- Social security will immediately return to its original state. If you didn't put anything in, you don't get anything out. Neither our President nor any other politician will be able to touch it.
- Welfare – Checks will be handed out on Fridays at the end of the 40 hour school week, and the successful completion of a urinalysis test and a passing grade in school.
- Professional Athletes – Steroids – The FIRST time you check positive, you are banned for life.
- Crime – We will adopt the Turkish method, the first time you steal, you lose your right hand.
- There are no more life sentences for murder. If convicted, you will be put to death by the same method you chose for your victim; gun, knife, strangulation, etc.
- One export will be allowed; Wheat, The world needs to eat. A bushel of wheat will be the exact same price as a barrel of oil.
- All foreign aid using American taxpayer money will immediately cease, and the saved money will pay off the national debt and ultimately lower your taxes. When disasters occur around the world, we'll ask the American people if they want to donate to a disaster fund, and each citizen can make the decision whether or not it is a worthy cause.
- The Pledge of Allegiance will be said every day at school and every day in Congress. It will include 'Under God' and 'Under God' will also be shown on all currency.
- The National Anthem will be played at all appropriate ceremonies, sporting events, outings ,etc.
- Prayers will be allowed in schools.

Rallies:

It was pointed out on TV by a Democratic operative that when Obama held a rally, 25-30,000 people showed up, whereas when McCain held one, he only drew 10-15,000 people.

The Republican spokesman replied, "That's because McCain's supporters are at work."

ONE Billion is HOW Much?

Here is something thought provoking. (snopes.com agrees this e-mail is accurate).
The next time you hear a politician use the word "billion" in a casual manner, think about whether you want the ;politicians' spending your tax money.

A billion is a difficult number to comprehend, but one advertising agency did a good job of putting that figure into some perspective in one of its releases.

- A billion seconds ago it was 1959.
- A billion minutes ago Jesus was alive.
- A billion hours ago our ancestors were living in the Stone Age.
- A billion days ago no one walked on the earth on two feet.
- A billion dollars ago was only 8 hours and 20 minutes at the rate our government is spending it.

While this thought is still fresh in our brain, let's take a look at New Orleans – it's amazing what you can learn with some simple division.

Louisiana Senator, Mary Landrieu (D), asked the Congress for $250 Billion to rebuild New Orleans.

That's an interesting number- what does is cover?

- Well, if you are one of 484,674 residents of New Orleans, (every man, woman and child) you each get $516,528.

- Or, if you have one of the 188,251 homes in New Orleans, your home gets $1,329,787.   Or if you are a family of four, your family gets $2,066,012.

Washington D.C.!!..   Are all your calculators broken??????

Maybe everyone should just flood their houses, and then we can all be on easy street for the rest of our lives, and forget about working, paying taxes and all that other useless stuff.

From the LA Times?

- 40% of all workers in L.A. County (L.A. County has 10.2 million people) are working for cash and are not paying taxes. This is because they are predominantly illegal immigrants working without a green card.
- 95% of warrants for murder in Los Angeles are for illegal aliens.
- 75% of people on the most wanted list in Los Angeles are for illegal aliens.
- Over 2/3 of all births in Los Angeles County are to illegal alien Mexicans on Medi-Cal, whose births were paid for by taxpayer money.
- Nearly 35% of all inmates in California detention centers are Mexican Nationals here illegally.
- Over 300,000 illegal aliens in Los Angeles County are living in garages.

- The FBI reports half of all gang members in Los Angeles are most likely illegal aliens from south of the border.
- Nearly 60% of all occupants of HUD properties are illegal aliens.
- 21 radio stations in Los Angeles County are Spanish speaking.
- In Los Angeles County, 5.1 million people speak English, 3.9 million people speak Spanish.
- Less than 2% of illegal aliens are picking our crops, but 29% are on welfare. Over 70% of the United States' annual population growth (and over 90% of California, Florida and New York) results from illegal immigration. 29% of the inmates in federal prisons are illegal aliens.

Tick Removal Made Easy:

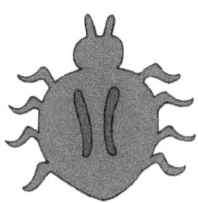

Apply a glob of liquid soap to a cotton ball. Cover the tick with the soap-soaked cotton ball and let it stay on the repulsive insect for a few seconds, (15-20), after which the tick will come out on its own and be stuck to the cotton ball when you lift it away. Unless someone is allergic to soap, I can't see that this would be damaging in any way. Happy tick hunting.

BUTTER VS MARGARINE:

If this is true, I'm switching to butter.
DID YOU KNOW THIS?

- Both butter and margarine have the same amount of calories.
- Butter is slightly higher in saturated fats at 8 grams compared to 5 grams in margarine.
- Eating margarine can increase heart disease by 53% as compared to eating the same amount of butter, according to a recent Harvard Medical Study.
- Eating butter increases the absorption of many other nutrients in other foods.
- Butter has many nutritional benefits where margarine has only a few, and only because they are added.
- Butter tastes much better than margarine, and it can enhance the flavors of other foods.
- Butter has been around for centuries whereas margarine has been around for less than 100 years.
- NOW FOR MARGARINE:
- Margarine is very high in Trans Fatty Acids.
- Margarine will triple the risk of Coronary Heart Disease.
- Margarine increases total and LDL cholesterol, (This is the bad cholesterol).

- Margarine lowers HDL cholesterol, (This is the good cholesterol).
- Margarine increases the risk of cancers by up to five fold.
- Margarine lowers the quality of breast milk.
- Margarine decreases immune response.
- Margarine decreases insulin response.
- And here is the most disturbing fact...Margarine is but ONE MOLECULE short of being PLASTIC. (This fact alone was enough to have me avoiding margarine for life, and anything else that is hydrogenated. Hydrogenated means that hydrogen is added, changing the molecular structure of food.)
- You can try this one yourself:
- Purchase a tub of margarine and leave it in your garage or a shaded area with the cover removed. Within a couple days your will note a few things.-no flies, not even those pesky fruit flies will go near it. (That should tell you something.) It does not rot or smell differently because it has no nutritional value. Nothing will grow on it. Even those teeny microorganisms cannot find a nutrient in which to grow. Why? Because margarine is nearly plastic. Would you melt your Tupperware and spread it on your toast?

Do you believe all this? Have your heard anything about margarine being THAT bad for you?

I think my "I Can't Believe it's Not Butter" is on the way to the trash can!

THIS ONE IS MY FAVORITE:

I bought a bird feeder. I hung it on my back porch and filled it with seed. Within a week we had hundreds of birds taking advantage of the continuous flow of free and easily accessible food. But then the birds started building nests in the boards of the patio, above the table, and next to the barbecue. Then came the poop. It was everywhere: on the patio tile, the chairs, the table ... and everywhere. Then some of the birds turned mean: They would dive bomb me and try to peck me even though I had fed them out of my own pocket. And other birds were boisterous and loud: They sat on the feeder and squawked and screamed at  all hours of the day and night and demanded that I fill the feeder when it got low on food. After a while, I couldn't even sit on my own patio anymore.

I took down the bird feeder and in three days the birds were gone. I cleaned up their mess and took down the many nests they had built all over the patio.

74

Soon, the back yard was like it used to be…Quiet, serene and no one demanding their rights to a free meal.

Now let's see …our government gives out free food, subsidized housing, free medical care, and free education and allows anyone born here to be an automatic citizen. Then the illegal immigrants came by the tens of thousands. Suddenly our taxes went up to pay for free services; small apartments began housing 5 families. Next, we have to wait 6 hours to be seen by an emergency room doctor, (if you can find one that is not bankrupt already): your child's 2nd grade class is behind other schools because over half the children can't speak English: Corn Flakes now come in a bilingual box; I have to press "one" to hear my bank talk to me in English, and people waving flags other than "Old Glory" are squawking and screaming in the streets, demanding more rights and free liberties.

Mr. President, maybe it's time for the government to take down the bird feeder…….

MOSQUITOES:

I have read that the best way of getting rid of mosquitoes is with Listerine, the original medicinal type. The Dollar Store-type works too. If you find yourself at a deck party and the pesky little critters are having a ball biting everybody, just spray the lawn and the deck floor with Listerine and the little demons will disappear. If you are at a picnic or in the park, you can spray around the picnic tables, the children's swing and slide area, and any standing water nearby. I'm told the results should last for a couple days. You can spray it around all your doors and windows. Don't spray it directly on your wooden door, (like your front door), but spray around the frame. Spray around the window frames and even inside the dog house if you have one.

I haven't tried this one yet but I definitely will sometime in the near future. Ed

Real Facts: At least that's what the e-mail said:

- Look at your zipper. Do you see the initials YKK? They stand for Yoshida Kogyo Kabushibibaisha, the world's largest zipper manufacturer.
- 40% of McDonald's profits come from the sales of Happy Meals.
- 315 entries in Webster's 1996 Dictionary were misspelled.
- On the average, 12 newborns will be given to the wrong parents daily.
- Chocolate kills dogs! This is true, chocolate affects a dog's heart and nervous system. A few ounces are enough to kill a small sized dog.
- Ketchup was sold in the 1830's as a medicine.
- Leonardo da Vinci could write with one hand and draw with the other at the same time.
- Because metal was scarce, the Oscars given out during World War II were made of wood.

- There are no clocks in the Las Vegas gambling casinos.
- Leonardo da Vinci invented scissors. Also, it took him 10 years to paint Mona Lisa's lips.
- Bruce Lee was so fast that they actually had to slow a film down so you could see his moves. That was just the opposite of the norm.
- The original name for the butterfly was "flutterby".
- By raising your legs slowly and lying on your back, you cannot sink in quicksand.
- Mosquito repellents don't repel. They hide you. The spray blocks the mosquitoes sensors so they don't know you are there.
- Michael Jordan made more money from Nike annually than the entire Nike factory workers in Malaysia combined.
- Marilyn Monroe had six toes on one foot.
- If Hitler's Mother seriously considered having an abortion, but was talked out of it by her Doctor.
- To escape the grip of a crocodile's jaws, prick your fingers into its eyeballs. It will let you go instantly.
- The average person falls asleep in seven minutes.
- The "pound" key (#) on your keyboard is called an octothorp.
- The only domesticated animal not mentioned in the Bible is the 'cat'.
- "Dreamt" is the only word in the English language that ends in "mt".
- It is impossible to sneeze with your eyes open.
- In Chinese, the KFC slogan "finger licken good" comes out as "eat your fingers off".
- A cockroach can live for ten days without its head.
- We shed 40 pounds of skin in our lifetime.
- Mexico City sinks about 10 inches every year.
- Brains are more active while sleeping than while watching Television.
- Blue is the favorite color of 80 percent of Americans.
- When a person shakes his head from side to side, he is saying "yes" in Sri Lanka.
- There are more chickens than people in the World.
- Your thumbnail grows the slowest, and your middle finger grows the fastest.
- There are more telephones than people in Washington D.C.
- The average four year old child asks over four hundred questions per day.
- The three wealthiest families in the world have more assets than the combined wealth of the forty-eight poorest nations.
- The world's youngest parents were 8 and 9 and lived in China in 1910.
- Our eyes remain the same size from birth onward, but our noses and ears never stop growing.
- You burn more calories sleeping than you do watching Television.

- A person will die from a total lack of sleep sooner than from starvation. Death will occur in   about 10 days without sleep, while starvation takes a few weeks.
- The painting of "Mona Lisa" has no eyebrows.
- When the moon is directly overhead, you weigh slightly less.
- Alexander Graham Bell, the inventor of the telephone, never telephoned his Wife or Mother because they were both deaf.
- "I am." That is the shortest complete sentence in the English language.
- Colgate faces a big obstacle marketing their toothpaste in Spanish speaking countries because the word Colgate translates into the command, "go hang yourself."
- Like fingerprints, everyone's tongue print is different.
- "Bookkeeper", is the only word in the English language with three consecutive double letters.
- Right handed people live, on average, nine years longer than left handed people do.
- The sentence used in typing practice, "the quick brown fox jumps over the lazy dog" uses every Letter in the English language.
- Every human spent about half an hour as a single cell.
- An average person uses the bathroom 6 times per day.
- Babies are born with 300 bones, but by adulthood we have only 206 bones in our bodies.
- Beards are the fastest growing hairs on the human body. If the average man never trimmed his beard, it would grow to nearly 30 feet long in his lifetime.
- According to Genesis 1:20-22, the chicken came before the egg.
- The longest name for a place still in use is:
- Taumatawhakatangihangaoauauotameteaturi-
- pukakpikimaungahoronukupokaiwhenuakitanatahu. It's the name of a New Zealand hill.
- If you leave Tokyo by plane at 7:00 am, you will arrive in Honolulu at approximately 4:30 pm the previous day.
- Scientists in Australia's Parkes Observatory thought they had positive proof of alien life, when they began picking up radio-waves from space. However, after investigation, the radio emissions were traced to a Microwave Oven in the same building.
- Wearing headphones for an hour increases the bacteria in your ear 700 times.

Thomas Jefferson's Koran: An Article by Ted Sampley.

Keith Ellison, now officially the first Muslim United States congressman, placed his hand on the Koran, the Muslim book of jihad, and pledged his allegiance to the United States during his ceremonial swearing-in.

The Koran Ellison used once belonged to Thomas Jefferson, third president of the United States and one of America's founding fathers. Ellison borrowed it from the Rare Book Section of the Library of Congress. It is one of the 6,500 Jefferson books archived in the library.

Ellison, who was born in Detroit and converted to Islam while in college, said he chose to use Jefferson's Koran because it showed that "a visionary like Jefferson" believed wisdom could be gleaned from many sources.
Ellison was right about Jefferson believing wisdom could be "gleaned" from the Muslim Koran. At the time Jefferson owned the book, he needed to know everything possible about Muslims because he was about to advocate war against the Islamic "Barbary" states of Morocco, Algeria, Tunisia and Tripoli.

Ellison's use of Jefferson's Koran as a prop illuminates a subject once well-known in the history of the United States, but mostly forgotten today—the Muslim pirate slavers who enslaved millions of Africans and tens of thousands of Christian Europeans and Americans in the Islamic "Barbary" states.

Over the course of ten centuries, Muslim pirates cruised the African and Mediterranean coastline, pillaging villages and seizing slaves. It was typical of Muslim raiders to kill off as many older men and women as possible so the preferred "booty" of only young women and children would be collected.

Young non-Muslim women were targeted because of their value as concubines in Islamic markets. Islamic law provides for the sexual interests of Muslim men by allowing them to take as many as four wives, and to have as many concubines as their fortunes allow.

Boys as young as 9 or 10 were often mutilated to create eunuchs who would bring higher prices in the slave markets of the Middle East. It was estimated that only a small number of the boys subjected to the mutilation survived after the surgery.

When American colonists rebelled against British rule in 1776 and lost Royal Navy protection. American merchant ships were attacked and their Christian crews enslaved by Muslim pirates operating under the control of the "Dey of Algiers" – an Islamist warlord ruling Algeria.

The Continental Congress in 1784 appointed John Adams, Thomas Jefferson and Benjamin Franklin to negotiate treaties with the four Barbary States, agreeing to appease the Muslim slavers by paying tribute and ransoms in order to retrieve seized American ships and buy the freedom of enslaved sailors.

Adams argued in favor of paying tribute as the cheapest way to get American commerce in the Mediterranean moving again. Jefferson was apposed. He believed there would be no end to the demands for tribute and wanted matters settled "through the medium of war." He proposed a league of trading nations to force an end to Muslim piracy.

In 1786, Jefferson, then American ambassador to France, and Adams, then American ambassador to Britain, met in London to negotiate a peace treaty with Sidi Haji Abdul Rahman Adja, the "Dey of Algiers" ambassador to Britain. During the meeting, Jefferson and Adams asked the Dey's ambassador why Muslims held so much hostility towards America, a nation with which they had no previous contacts.

Later the two future presidents reported to the American Congress the ambassador's answer: that Islam "was founded on the Laws of their Prophet, that it was written in their Koran that all nations who should not have acknowledged their authority were sinners, that it was their right and duty to make war upon them wherever they could be found, to make slaves of all they could take as prisoners, and that every Muscleman (Muslim) who should be slain in battle was sure to go to paradise."

For the following 15 years, the American government paid the Muslims millions of dollars for the safe passage of American ships or the return of American hostages. The payments in ransom and tribute amounted to 20 percent of the United States government's annual revenues in 1800.

Not long after Jefferson's inauguration as president in 1801, he dispatched a group of frigates to defend American interests in the Mediterranean, and then informed Congress. He declared that America was going to spend "millions for defense, but not one cent for tribute." Jefferson pressed the issue by deploying American Marines and many of America's best warships to the Muslim Barbary Coast.

In 1805, American Marines marched across the desert from Egypt into Tripolitania, forcing the surrender of Tripoli and freeing all American slaves. During the Jefferson administration, the Muslim Barbary States, crumbling as a result of intense American naval bombardment and on-shore raids by Marines, finally officially agreed to abandon slavery and piracy.

Jefferson's victory over the Muslims lives on today in the Marine Hymn, *"From the halls of Montezuma to the shores of Tripoli."*

It wasn't until 1815 that the problem was fully settled by the total defeat of all the Muslim slave-trading pirates. Jefferson had been right. The "medium of war" was the only way to put an end to the Muslim problem. Mr. Ellison was right about Jefferson – he was a "visionary" wise enough to read and learn about the enemy from their own Muslim book of jihad.

This Is A MUST Read For Everyone:

Check the expiration date on all of your packages like pancakes and cake mixes that have yeast included in the package. Over time the yeast will develop spores that will do you great harm if not kill you. So, throw away all outdated boxes immediately if not sooner.

A few dollars for a box of outdated pancake mix is not worth throwing your life away. Please pass this on to the rest of your family and to all your friends. This is very important.

Are You A Democrat, Republican or Red Neck? Here's The Tell Tale Test:

The answer can be found by answering the following question:

You are walking down a deserted street with your Wife and two small children at your side.

Suddenly, a huge mean looking character comes around the corner with a very large knife.

He locks eyes with you, screams obscenities, raises the knife and charges at you.

You are carrying a Colt 1911 cal. 45 Semi-Automatic Handgun and you are an expert shot.

You have mere seconds before he reaches you and your family. What do you do?

Democrat's Answer:

- Well, that's not enough information to answer the question.
- Does the man look poor or oppressed?
- Have I ever done anything to him that would inspire him to attack me?
- Could we run away?
- What does my Wife think?
- Could I possibly swing my gun like a club and knock the knife out of his hand? What does the law say about this kind of situation?
- Does my gun have appropriate safety built into it?
- Why am I carrying a loaded gun anyway, and what kind of message does this send to society and to my children?
- Is it possible he'd be happy with just killing me?
- Does he definitely want to kill me, or would he be satisfied with just taking my money?

- If I were to grab his knees and hold on, could my Wife and kids get away while he was stabbing me?
- Should I call 911?
- Why is this street so deserted?
- We need to raise taxes, have a paint and weed day and make this a happier, healthier street that would discourage such behavior.
- This is all so confusing!
- I need to debate this with some friends for a few days and try to come to a consensus...

Republican's Answer: BANG!!!

Redneck's Answer:

- BANG, BANG, BANG, BANG, BANG, BANG
- Click....Sounds of reloading...
- BANG, BANG, BANG, BANG, BANG, BANG
- Click.
- Daughter: "Nice grouping, Daddy! Were those the Winchester Silver Tips or the Hollow Points?"
- Son: "Can I shoot the next one, Dad?"
- Wife: "You aren't taking that one to the taxidermist"!

Words of Wisdom:

- People who can hold their tongues rarely have any trouble holding their friends.
- A man is not really poor if he can still laugh.
- The man who thinks he knows it all has merely stopped thinking.
- If the world laughs at you, laugh right back. It is as funny as you are.
- Ability without ambition is like a car without a motor.
- Ability will enable a man to get to the top, but it takes character to keep him there.
- You cannot make a place for yourself under the sun if you keep sitting in the shade of the family tree.
- Adversity is the only diet that will reduce a 'fat head'.
- We learn some things from prosperity, but we learn many more things from adversity.
- Education is an ornament in prosperity and a refuge in adversity.
- Age is what makes furniture worth more and people worth less.
- What do you suppose ages faster, whiskey or the man who drinks it?

- Sixty five is the age when one acquires sufficient experience to lose his job.
- Some girls get married for financial security: others get divorced for the same reason.
- The more arguments you win, the fewer friends you will have.
- It is impossible to defeat an ignorant man in an argument.
- Discussion is an exchange of knowledge: argument is an exchange of ignorance.
- People who know the least always argue the most.

Your Vote Is Important:

- In 1645 one vote gave Oliver Cromwell control of England.
- In 1649 one vote caused Charles I of England to be executed.
- In 1776 one vote gave America the English language instead of German.
- In 1839 one vote elected Marcus Morton Governor of Massachusetts.
- In 1845 one vote brought Texas into the Union.
- In 1868 one vote saved President Andrew Johnson from impeachment.
- In 1876 one vote gave Rutherford B. Hayes the Presidency of the United States.
- In 1876 one vote changed France from a monarchy to a Republic.
- How important is one vote?

Your vote could make the difference.

ICE: In Case of Emergency: This could save someone a lot of frustration.

We all carry a mobile phone with names and numbers stored in its memory but nobody, other than ourselves, knows which of these numbers belong to our closest family members or friends.

If we were to be involved in an accident or were taken ill, the people attending us would have our mobile phone but wouldn't know who to call.

They wouldn't know who to call in case of emergency, hence the term 'ICE' (In Case of Emergency).

You can put the number or numbers under the name of the person or persons you need to have notified In Case of Emergency.

The Prime person would be listed under ICE-1 and the second person could be listed under ICE-2 '*and so forth and so on'.

If this idea caught on nationally, it would change how emergency personnel handled the need to notify victim's relatives and/or friends during an emergency situation.

Emergency Service Personnel and hospital staff would be able to quickly contact the right person by simply dialing the number you have stored as 'ICE'.

P.S. I've always wanted to say that phrase, 'and so forth and so on' but it didn't fit in anywhere during my engineering career. Ed

I Know This Is Long, But You Need To Read It:

Dear Mr. Ex-President Clinton:

I recently saw a bumper sticker that said, "Thank me, I voted for Clinton-Gore." So, I sat down and reflected on that, and I am sending my "Thank You" for what you have done, specifically:

- Thank you for introducing us to Jennifer Flowers, Paula Jones, Monica Lewinsky, Dolly Kyle Browning, Kathleen Willey and Juanita Broderick. Did I leave anyone out?

- Thank you for teaching my 8 year old about oral sex. I had really planned to wait until he was a little older to discuss it with him, but now he knows more about it than I did as a senior in college.

- Thank you for showing us that sexual harassment in the work place (especially in the White House) and on the job is quite OK, and all you have to know is what the meaning of "it" is. It really is great to know that certain sexual acts are not really sex, and that one person may have sex while the other one does NOT have sex.

- Thank you for re-introducing the concept of impeachment to a new generation and demonstrating that the ridiculous plot of the movie "Wag the Dog" could be plausible after all.

- Thanks for making Jimmy Carter look competent, Gerald Ford look graceful, Richard Nixon look honest, Lyndon Johnson look truthful and John Kennedy look moral.

- Thank you for the 73 House and Senate witnesses who have pled the 5th Amendment and the 17 witnesses who have fled the country to avoid having to testify about Democratic campaign fund raising.

- Thank you for the 19 charges, 8 convictions and 4 imprisonment's from the Whitewater "mess" and the 55 criminal charges and 32 criminal convictions in the other "Clinton" scandals.

- Thanks also for reducing our military by half, "gutting" much of our foreign policy, and flying all over the world on "vacations" carefully disguised as necessary trips.

- Thank you also, for "finding" millions of dollars (We really didn't need it in the first place, and I can't think of a more deserving group of recipients for our hard earned tax dollars) for all your globetrotting. I understand you, the family and your associates have logged more time aboard Air Force One than any other administration.

- Now that you've left the White House, thanks for the 140 pardons of convicted felons and indicted felons-in-exile. We will love to have them rejoin society. (Not to mention the scores you pardoned while Governor of Arkansas).

- Thanks also for removing the White House silverware. I'm sure that Laura Bush didn't like the pattern anyway.

- Thanks to you and your staff in the West Wing of the White House for vandalizing and destroying government property on the way out. I also appreciate the removal of all that excess weight (china, silverware, linen, towels, ash trays, soap, pens, magnetic compass, flight manuals, etc.) out of Air Force One. The weight savings means the burning less fuel, thus less tax dollars spent on jet fuel. Thanks again.

And Bill, please make sure that Hillary enjoys the $8 million dollar advance for her "tell-all" book and you, Bill, the $10 million dollar advance for your memoirs. Who says crime doesn't pay?

And the rest of the story:

Hillary Rodham Clinton, as a New York State Senator, now comes under the "Congressional Retirement and Staffing Plan," which means that even if she never gets re-elected, she STILL receives her Congressional salary for the rest of her life. (Wouldn't it be nice if all Americans were pension eligible after only 4 years?) If Bill outlives her, he then inherits HER salary for the rest of HIS life. He is already getting his Presidential salary for the rest of his life. If Hillary outlives Bill, she also gets HIS salary for the rest of HER life. Guess who pays for that?

The American Taxpayer!

It's common knowledge that in order for Hillary to establish NY residency, she and Bill purchased a million dollar plus house in upscale Chappaqua, New York. That makes sense. They are entitled to Secret Service protection for life. Still makes sense. Here is where it becomes interesting. Their mortgage payments hover at around $10,000 per month. BUT, an extra residence HAD to be built within the acreage to house the Secret Service agents. So, the Clintons charge the Federal government $10,000 monthly rent for the use of that extra residence, which is just about equal to their mortgage payment. This means that we, the taxpayers, are paying the Clinton's salary, mortgage, transportation, safety and security, as well as the salaries for their 12 man staff, and this is all perfectly legal. Work hard and pay your taxes everybody...

BILL CLINTON'S MILITARY CAREER:

Sept. 08, 1964 Bill Clinton registered for the draft accepting all contractual conditions of registering for the draft. His **Selective Service # was 3 26 46 228.**
Nov. 17, 1964 Bill Clinton was classified 2-S.
Mar. 20, 1968 Bill Clinton was re-classified 1-A.
July 28, 1969 Bill Clinton was ordered to report for induction. Bill Clinton refused to report and is not inducted into the military.
Aug. 07, 1969 Bill Clinton was reclassified 1-D after enlisting in the United States Army Reserves under the authority of COL. E. Holmes.
Sept. 1969 Bill Clinton signs enlistment papers and takes the oath of enlistment. However, Bill Clinton fails to report to his duty station at the University of Arkansas ROTC.
Oct. 30, 1969 Bill Clinton is reclassified 1-A as enlistment with the Army Reserves is revoked by Colonel E Holmes and Clinton is now AWOL and subject to arrest under **Public Law 90-40 (2)(a) registrant who has** failed to report...remains liable for induction.
Dec. 01, 1969 Bill Clinton's birth date lottery number, (311) is drawn, but anyone who has already been ordered to report for induction is INELIGIBLE.
1974 Bill Clinton runs for Congress while a fugitive from justice under Public Law 90-40.
1976 Bill Clinton runs for Arkansas Attorney General while a fugitive from justice.
Jan. 21, 1977 Bill Clinton receives a pardon from President Carter.

Bill Clinton becomes the **FIRST PARDONED FEDERAL FELON** ever to serve as President of the United States.

All these statements are alleged to be true and are from the Freedom of Information requests, public laws and various books that have been published and have not been refuted by Bill Clinton.

After the 1993 World Trade Center bombing, President Clinton promised that those responsible would be hunted down and punished.

After the 1995 bombing in Saudi Arabia, which killed five U.S. military personnel, Clinton promised that those responsible would be hunted down and punished.

After the 1996 Khobar Towers bombing in Saudi Arabia which killed 19 and injured 200 U.S. military personnel, Clinton promised that those responsible would be hunted down and punished.
After the 1998 bombing of the U.S. embassies in Africa, which killed 224 and injured 5,000, Clinton promised that those responsible would be hunted down and punished.

After the 2000 bombing of the USS Cole, which killed 17 and injured 39 U.S. Sailors, Clinton promised that those responsible would be hunted down and punished.

Maybe if Clinton had kept those promises, an estimated 3,000 people in New York and Washington D.C. who are now dead would be alive today.

This is en e-mail That Is Hard For Me To Read.

I just can't bring myself to believe this is true. It's a long stretch for me, but, I have to include it.

This is supposedly a list of Clinton friends/associates that met with untimely and strange deaths.

1. **James McDougal** – James was Clinton's convicted Whitewater partner who died of an apparent heart attack, while in solitary confinement. He was a key witness in Ken Starr's investigation.

2. **Mary Mahoney** – Mary was a former White House intern who was murdered July 1997 at a Starbuck's Coffee Shop in Georgetown. The murder happened just before she was to go public with her story of sexual harassment in the White House.
3. **Vince Foster** – Vince was a Former White House counselor, and colleague of Hillary Clinton at Little Rock's Rose Law Firm, he died of a gunshot wound to the head, ruled a suicide.
4. **Ron Brown** – Ron was the Secretary of Commerce and former DNC Chairman. He was reported to have died by impact in a plane crash. A pathologist close to the investigation reported that there was a hole in the top of Brown's skull resembling a gunshot wound. At the time of his

death Brown was being investigated, and spoke publicly of his willingness to cut a deal with prosecutors. The rest of the people on the plane also died. A few days later the Air Traffic controller committed suicide.

5. **C. Victor Raiser II** – Raiser was a major player in the Clinton fund raising organization who died in a private plane crash in July 1992.

6. **Paul Tulley** – Paul was the Democratic National Committee Political Director and was found dead in a hotel room in Little Rock, in September of 1992. He was described by Clinton as a "Dear friend and trusted advisor".

7. **Ed Willey** – Ed was a Clinton fund raiser, and was found dead November 1993 deep in the woods of VA of a gunshot wound to the head. It was ruled as a suicide. Ed Willey died on the same day his Wife Kathleen Willey claimed Bill Clinton groped her in the oval office in the White House. Ed Willey was involved in several Clinton fund raising events.

8. **Jerry Parks** – Jerry was head of Clinton's gubernatorial security team in Little Rock. He was gunned down in his car at a deserted intersection outside of Little Rock. Park's Son said his Father was building a dossier on Clinton. He allegedly threatened to reveal his information. After he died the files were mysteriously removed from his house.

9. **James Bunch** – James died from a gunshot which was deemed a suicide. It was reported that James had a "Black Book" of people which contained names of influential people who visited prostitutes in Texas and Arkansas.

10. **James Wilson** – James was found dead in May 1993 from an apparent hanging suicide. He was reported to have ties to Whitewater.

11. **Kathy Ferguson** – Kathy was the ex-wife of Arkansas Trooper Danny Ferguson and was found dead in May 1994 in her living room with a gunshot to her head. It was ruled a suicide even though there were several packed suitcases, as if she were going somewhere. Danny Ferguson was a co-defendant, along with Bill Clinton in the Paula Jones lawsuit. Kathy Ferguson was a possible corroborating witness for Paula Jones.

12. **Bill Shelton** – Bill was an Arkansas State Trooper and fiancée of Kathy Ferguson. After being critical of the suicide ruling of his fiancée, he was found dead at the grave site of his fiancée in June 1994 of a gunshot wound also ruled as a suicide.

13. **Gandy Baugh** – Gandy was the attorney for Clinton's friend Dan Lassater, and died by jumping out of a window of a tall building in January, 1994. His client was a convicted drug distributor.

14. **Florence Martin** – Florence was an accountant and sub-contractor for the CIA, and was related to the Barry Seal Mena Airport drug smuggling case. He died of three gunshot wounds.

15. **Suzanne Coleman** – Suzanne reportedly had an affair with Clinton when he was Arkansas Attorney General. She died of a gunshot wound

to the back of the head, ruled a suicide. She was pregnant at the time of her death.

16.   **Paula Grober** – Paula was Clinton's speech interpreter for the deaf from 1978 until her death on December 9, 1992. She died in a one car accident.

17.   **Danny Casolaro** – Danny was an investigating reporter, investigating Mena Airport and the Arkansas Development Finance Authority. Danny slit his wrists, apparently, in the middle of his investigation.

18.   **Paul Wilcher** – Paul was an attorney investigating corruption at Mena Airport with Casolaro and the 1980 "October Surprise". He was found dead on a toilet on June 22, 1993 in his Washington DC apartment. He had delivered a report to Janet Reno 3 weeks before his death.

19.   **Jon Parnell Walker** – Jon Parnell was a Whitewater investigator for the Resolution Trust Corporation. He jumped to his death from his Arlington, Virginia apartment balcony on August 15, 1993. He was investigating the Morgan Guaranty scandal.

20.   **Barbara Wise** – Barbara was a Commerce Department staffer. She worked closely with Ron Brown and John Huang. The cause of her death is unknown. She died on November 29, 1996. Her bruised, nude body was found locked in her office at the Department of Commerce.

21.   **Charles Meissner** – Charles was the Assistant Secretary of Commerce who gave John Huang special security clearance, and he died shortly thereafter in a small plane crash.

22.   **Dr. Stanley Heard** – Dr. Heard was the Chairman of the National Chiropractic Health Care Advisory Committee. He died with his attorney, Steve Dickson in a small plane crash. Dr Heard, in addition to serving on Clinton's advisory council personally treated Clinton's Mother, Stepfather and Brother.

23.   **Barry Seal** – Barry was a drug running pilot out of Mena Arkansas, his death was not an accident.

24.   **Johnny Lawhorn Jr.** – Johnny was a mechanic who found a check made out to Bill Clinton in the trunk of a car left at his repair shop. He was found dead after his car had hit a utility pole.

25.   **Stanley Huggins** – Stanley investigated Madison Guaranty. His death was a purported suicide and his report was never released.

26.   **Hershell Huggins** – Hershell was an attorney and Clinton fund raiser who died March 1, 1994 when his airplane exploded.

27.   **Kevin Ives and Don Henry** – Known as the "The Boys on The Track" case. Reports say the boys may have stumbled upon the Mena Arkansas airport drug operation. A controversial case, the initial report of death said, "death due to falling asleep on railroad tracks. Later reports claim the 2 boys had been slain before being placed on the tracks. Many linked to the case died before their testimony could come before a Grand Jury.

THE FOLLOWING PERSONS HAD INFORMATION ON THE IVES/HENRY CASE:

1. **Keith Coney** – Keith died when his motorcycle slammed into the back of a truck in July 1988.
2. **Keith McMaskle** – Keith died after being stabbed 113 times in November 1988.
3. **Gregory Collins** – Gregory died from a gunshot wound in January 1989.
4. **Jeff Rhodes** – Jeff was shot, mutilated and found burned in a trash dump in April 1989.
5. **James Milan** – James was found decapitated. However, the Coroner ruled his death was due to "natural causes".
Jordan Kettleson – Jordan was found shot to death in the front seat of his pickup truck in June 1990.
6. **Richard Winters** – Richard was a suspect in the Ives/Henry deaths. He was killed in a set-up robbery in July 1989.

THE FOLLOWING CLINTON BODYGUARDS ARE NOW DEAD:

1. Major William S. Barkley Jr.
2. Captain Scott J. Reynolds.
3. Sgt. Brian Hanley.
4. Sgt. Tim Sabel...
5. Major General William Robertson.
6. Col. William Densberger.
7. Col. Robert Kelly.
8. Spec. Gary Rhodes.
9. Steve Willis.
10. Robert Williams.
11. Conway LeBleu.
12. Todd McKeehan.

This is quite an impressive list. I hope we have seen the end of the list. I put in many hours of thought on whether to include this story or not.

I thought the story was intriguing but any accusation against the Clintons in regards to the deaths of all these people is way beyond ridiculous in my way of thinking. And what do you think?

809 Area Code

This is very important information provided to us by AT&T.

DON'T EVER DIAL AREA CODE 809.

This one is being distributed all throughout the USA. This is pretty scary stuff. Especially given the way they try to get you to call. They get you to call by leaving a message on your phone late at night telling you that it is information about a family member who is been ill or to tell you someone has been arrested, died or to let you know you have won a wonderful prize, etc.

In each case, you are told to call the 809 number right away. Since there are so many new area codes these days, people unknowingly return these calls.

If you call from the US you will apparently be charged $2425 per minute. You will possibly get a long recorded message. The point is they will try to keep you on the phone as long as possible to increase the charges.

WHY IT WORKS:

The 809 area code is located in the Dominican Republic.

The charges afterward can become a real nightmare. That's because you actually did make the call. If you complain, both your local phone company and your long distance carrier will not want to get involved and will most likely tell you that they are simply providing the billing for the foreign company.

You will end up dealing with a foreign company argues they have done nothing wrong.

AT&T VERIFIES THAT IT IS TRUE:
http://www.att.com/gen/press-room?pid=6045

SNOPES VERIFIES THAT IT IS TRUE:
http:/www.snopes.com/fraud/telephone/809.asp

GENERAL DWIGHT EISENHOWER:

It is a matter of history that when the Supreme Commander of the Allied Forces, General Dwight Eisenhower, found the victims of the Nazi death camps he ordered all possible photographs to be taken, and for the German people from surrounding villages to be ushered through the camps and even be made to bury the dead.

He did this because he said in words to this effect: "Get all this on record now – get the films – get the witnesses – because somewhere down the road of history some bastard will get up and say that this never happened. This week, the UK debated whether to remove the Holocaust from its school curriculum because it 'offends' the Muslim population which claims it never occurred.

It is not removed as of this writing; however, this is a frightening portent of the fear that is gripping the world and how easily each country is giving in to it. It is now nearly 70 years after the Second World War in Europe ended.

Now more than ever, with Iran among others, claiming the Holocaust to be a 'myth,' it is imperative to make sure the world never forgets. How many years will it be before the attack on the world trade center - "NEVER HAPPENED"

Cell Phone Numbers:

Cell phone numbers went public last March. All cell phone numbers were released to the telemarketers.

You will be charged for any calls made to your cell phone. To prevent this, call the following number from your cell phone: 888-382-1222.

This is the National DO NOT CALL listing. It will only take a minute of your time. It blocks your number for 5 (five) years. You must call from the cell phone that you want to have blocked.

http:/www.donotcall.gov/default.aspx

The title of this section is: HOW DID JEFFERSON KNOW????

Here are a few of his quotes:

- When we get piled upon one another in large cities, as in Europe, we shall become as corrupt as Europe.
- The democracy will cease to exist when you take away from those who are willing to work and give to those who would not.
- It is incumbent on every generation to pay its own debts as it goes. A principle which if acted upon would save one-half of the wars of the world.
- I predict future happiness for Americans if they can prevent the government from wasting the labors of the people under the pretense of taking care of them.
- My reading of history convinces me that most bad government results from too much government.
- No free man shall ever be debarred the use of arms.
- The strongest reason for the people to retain the right to keep and bear arms is, as a last resort, to protect themselves against tyranny in government.
- The tree of liberty must be refreshed from time to time with the blood of patriots and tyrants.

- To compel man to subsidize with his taxes the propagation of ideas which he disbelieves and abhors in sinful and tyrannical.
- Thomas Jefferson said in 1802: "I believe that banking institutions are more dangerous to our liberties than standing armies. If the American people ever allow private banks to control the issue of their currency, first by inflation, then by deflation, the banks and corporations that will grow up around the banks will deprive the people of all property – until their children wake-up homeless on the continent their fathers conquered".

Google Information

This is something you will want to have and use. I still remember when the telephone company charged me $1.50 to get a phone number from 411 information.

My compliments to Google! Just leave it up to Google to come up with something like this!!

Here's a number worth putting in your cell phone, or your home phone speed dial. 1-800-goog411 or 1-800-466-4411.

This is an awesome service from Google, and it's free – great when you are on the road.

Don't waste your money on 411 information calls and don't waste your time manually dialing the number. I am driving along in my car and I need to call the golf course and I don't know the number. I hit the Google speed dial for information that I have programmed.

The voice at the other end says, "City and State." I say, "Garland, Texas." He says, "Business, Name or Type of Service." I say, "Firewheel Golf Course." He says, "Connecting" and Firewheel answers the phone. How great is that? This is nationwide and it is absolutely free!

Click on the link below and watch the short clip for a quick demonstration:

http://www.google.com/goog411
http://www.google.com/goog411/>

Our Government at Rest:

If this story is true, it is so bizarre it's like a soap opera. Funny but alarming, considering how much authority they say they have! This needs to be passed on far and wide, media too. This probably can be verified on YouTube – search for the talk radio host.

It's unbelievable but, then that's the Government – and they want to run Health Care!

YOU ARE GONNA LOVE THIS:

How good is our government? A local talk show host, Ed Henley on 700AM radio was talking about how yesterday he decided he would make some calls to Washington DC to see if our government was prepared for the storm (not like they didn't have any warning). First he called the HQ for Homeland Security. Guess what! The phone rang for 3 minutes and no one answered, (He recorded the calls he made all day long by the way). He called again and someone did answer to tell him no one was there it was closed down because of the weather. Homeland Security HQ was down? No phone call forwarding? No answering system in place? No contingency plan for this type of situation? I feel safe now!!!

Then Ed decides to contact FEMA. Ed has a daughter in DC and thought, suppose she was snowed in without power. What would she do? Now FEMA is all in Washington DC, all 3,700 of them. And FEMA is the Federal EMERGENCY Management Assistance! Since their offices were closed, they were without power, (no backup generators?). His call was forwarded to a switchboard in VA. The switchboard operator said the offices were closed because of the storm and loss of power and all she knew was the governor of Washington DC would have to declare a state of emergency and ask the President for help.

What is wrong with this picture? (Hint-what state is Washington DC in?).

That's right, they don't have a governor. Ed is then transferred to the disaster relief group and is told the same. All Washington DC government offices are closed because of the blizzard. So the government branch responsible for handling disasters and preparedness is incapable of doing their job in DC? Oh, but it gets better

Ed then wonders if all businesses in DC are closed. So he finds a Holiday Inn three blocks from the capital building and calls. Guess what! Not only are they open, their restaurant is open and serving full meals. They have a full staff on duty including maid service.

AND THE FEMA FOLKS ARE STAYING THERE....

The new one is out! You might be a redneck if:

- You come back from the dump with more than you took.
- You take your dog for a walk and you both use the same tree.
- You can entertain yourself for more than 15 minutes with a flyswatter.
- Your boat has not left the driveway in 15 years.
- You burn your yard rather than mow it.
- You think "the Nutcracker" is a vise on the work bench.
- The Salvation Army won't take your furniture.
- You offer to give someone the shirt off your back and they don't want it.
- You have the local taxidermist on speed dial.
- You keep a can of raid on your kitchen table.
- Your Wife can climb a tree faster than your cat.
- Your Grandmother has "ammo" on her Christmas list.
- You keep flea and tick soap in the shower.
- You've been involved in a custody fight over a hunting dog.
- You go to the stock car races and don't need a program.
- You know how many bales of hay your car will hold.
- You have a rag for a gas cap.
- Your house doesn't have curtains but your truck does.
- You wonder how service stations keep their restrooms so clean.
- You can spit without opening your mouth.
- You consider your license plate personalized because your Father made it.
- Your lifetime goal is to own a fireworks stand.
- You have a complete set of salad bowls and they all say "Cool Whip" on the side.
- The biggest city you've ever been to is WalMart.
- Your working TV sits on top of your non-working TV.
- You've used your ironing board as a buffet table.
- A tornado hits your neighborhood and does $100,000.00 worth of improvements.
- You've used a toilet brush to scratch your back.
- You missed your fifth grade graduation because you were on jury duty.
- You think fast food is hitting a deer at 65 mph.

Snopes validates the facts below:

Past Speaker of the House Nancy Pelosi's home district includes San Francisco. Star-Kist Tuna's headquarters are in San Francisco, Pelosi's home district. Star-Kist is owned by Del Monte Foods and is a major contributor to Pelosi.

Star-Kist is the major employer in American Samoa, employing 75% of the Samoan work force.

Paul Pelosi, Nancy's Husband, owns $17,000,000,00 dollars of Star-Kist stock. In January, 2007 when the minimum wage was increased from $5.15 to $7.25 per hour, Pelosi had American Samoa exempted from the increase so Del Monte would not have to pay the higher wage.

This would make Del Monte products less expensive than that of its competitors.

When the huge bailout bill was passed, Pelosi added an earmark to the final bill adding $33,000,000.00 dollars for an "economic development credit in American Samoa".

Pelosi has called the Bush Administration "CORRUPT" and many other things!!! How do you spell "HYPOCRISY"? SHE"S SHAMELESS!!!

So Who Alerted The White House?

What is great, is the fact that George W. Bush heard about Fort Hood, got into his car and without any escort, (apparently his escort didn't have time to react), and drove to Fort Hood.

He was stopped at the main gate and the guard could not believe who he had just stopped.

Bush only asked for directions to the hospital then drove on. The gate guard announced that "The president is on the premises and is driving to the hospital". The whole base assumed it was Obama and went crazy looking for him.

When they discovered that it was Bush instead, they immediately offered him escort and Bush simply told them to shut up and let him visit the wounded and the dependents of the dead. Bush stayed at the fort for over six hours and was finally asked to leave by a message from the White House.

Obama flew in days later and held a "Photo" session in a gym and did not even go near the hospital. All this I picked up from two soldiers here who happened to be at Fort Hood when it all happened.

How To Fix The US Economy.

There recently was an article in the St. Petersburg, FL. Times. The Business Section asked readers for ideas on: "How Would You Fix the Economy?"

Here's one that I think nailed it:

Instead of giving Billions of dollars to companies that will squander the money on lavish parties and unearned bonuses, use the following plan. You can call it the "Patriotic Retirement Plan".

There are about 40 million people over 50 in the American work force.

- Pay them $1,000,000.00 each as a severance for early retirement with the following stipulations:

- They MUST retire. Forty million job openings – Unemployment fixed.

- They must buy a new American CAR. Forty million cars ordered – Auto Industry fixed.

- They MUST either buy a house or pay off their mortgage – Housing Crisis fixed.
- It can't get any easier than that!!

P.S. If more money is needed, have all members in Congress pay their taxes.

Mr. President, while you are at it, Make Congress retire on Social Security and Medicare. I'll bet both programs would be fixed pronto.

How They Vote In The United Nations:

- Kuwait votes AGAINST the United States 67% of the time.
- Qatar votes AGAINST the United States 57% of the time
- Morocco votes AGAINST the United States 70% of the time.
- United Arab Emirates votes AGAINST the United States 70% of the time.
- Jordan votes AGAINST the United States 71% of the time.
- Tunisia votes AGAINST the United States 71% of the time.
- Saudi Arabia votes AGAINST the United States 73% of the time.
- Yemen votes AGAINST the United States 74% of the time.
- Algeria votes AGAINST the United States 74% of the time.

- Oman votes AGAINST the United States 74% of the time.
- Sudan votes AGAINST the United States 75% of the time.
- Pakistan votes AGAINST the United States 75% of the time.
- Libya votes AGAINST the United States 76% of the time.
- Egypt votes AGAINST the United States 79% of the time.
- Lebanon votes AGAINST the United States 80% of the time.
- India votes AGAINST the United States 81% of the time.
- Syria votes AGAINST the United States 84% of the time.
- Mauritania votes AGAINST the United States 87% of the time.
- AND HERE"S THE FUN PART:
- Egypt still receives $2,000,000,000.00 annually in U.S. Foreign Aid.
- Jordan receives $192,814,000.00 annually in U.S. Foreign Aid.
- Pakistan receives $6,721,000.00 annually in U.S. Foreign Aid.
- India receives $143,699,000.00 annually in U.S. Foreign Aid.

Perhaps it is time to get out of the United Nations and give the tax savings back to the American Citizens who are skimping and just getting by.

This is Disgusting and Unacceptable!!!!!!!

This is a New Political Party, Not Democrat, Not Republican, and Not Independent:

It's called the "Pissed Off Party" (or 'POP')

This party is dedicated to vote every incumbent out of office as soon as possible. If you are a Democrat, vote Democrat. Just don't vote for an incumbent. If you are a Republican, vote Republican. Just don't vote for an incumbent.

We need to send message to all politicians, that we are tired of all their B.S. If the whole country votes out all the incumbents, the new incoming politicians will get the message too.

The U.S. Postal Service was established in 1775. You have had 239 years to get it right and it is broke.

Social Security was established in 1935. You have had 79 years to get it right and it is broke.

Fannie Mae was established in 1938. You have had 76 years to get it right and it is broke.

War on Poverty started in 1964. You have had 50 years to get it right; $ 1 trillion of our money is confiscated each year and transferred to "the poor" and they only want more.

Medicare and Medicaid were established in 1970. You have had 44 years to get them right and they are broke.

Freddie Mac was established in 1970. You have had 44 years to get it right and it is broke.

The Department of Energy was created in 1977 to lesson our dependence on foreign oil. It has ballooned to 16,000 employees with a budget of $24 billion dollars a year and we import more oil than ever before. You had 37 years to get it right and it is an abysmal failure.

You have FAILED in every "government Service" you have shoved down our throats while overspending our tax dollars.
AND YOU WANT AMERICANS TO BELIEVE YOU CAN BE TRUSTED WITH A GOVERNMENT – RUN HEALTH CARE SYSTEM?

IT'S NOT ABOUT THE NEED FOR GOOD HEALTH CARE, IT'S ABOUT TRUSTING THE GOVERNMENT TO RUN IT.

General Electric:

When companies know they are about to be taxed to death they leave the country. As we all know, corporations have no loyalty. It's all about the bottom line. You would think our president would know this.

General Electric is planning to move its 115 year old X-ray division from Waukesha, Wisconsin to Beijing, China. In addition to moving the headquarters, the company will invest $2 billion in China and train more than 65 engineers and create six research centers.

This is the same GE that made $5.1 billion in the United States last year, but paid no taxes. This is the same company that employs more people overseas than it does in the United States.

So, let me get this straight. President Obama appointed GE Chairman Jeff Immelt to head his commission on job creation (job czar). Immelt is supposed to help create jobs.

I guess the President forgot to tell him in which country he was supposed to be creating those jobs.

Entitlements my butt...what the devil is wrong with Congress:

Remember, not only did you contribute to Social Security but your employer did too. It totaled 15% of your income before taxes. If you averaged only $30 thousand a year over your working life, that's close to $220,500.

If you calculate the future value of $4,500 per year, (yours and your employer's contribution) at a simple 5% (that's less than what the government pays on the money that it borrows), after 49 years of working (that was me), you would have $892,919.98.

If you took out only 3% per year, you would receive $26,787.60 per year and it would last better than 30 years (until you were 95 if you retired at the age of 65) and that is with no interest paid on that final amount on deposit.

If you bought an annuity and it paid 4% per year, you would have a lifetime income of $2,976.40 per month.

Washington has pulled off a bigger Ponzi scheme than Bernie Madhoff ever had. Entitlement my butt, I paid cash for my social security insurance... Just because Congress borrowed the money, doesn't make my benefits some kind of charity or handout.

Congressional benefits are; free healthcare, outrageous retirement packages, 67 paid holidays, three weeks paid vacation, unlimited paid sick days, now that's welfare, and they have the nerve to call my social security retirement entitlements?

Charlie Reese's final column, A Great Read:

This is Charlie Reese's final column for the Orlando Sentinel. He has been a journalist for 49 years. He is retiring and this is HIS LAST COLUMN.

This is about as clear and easy to understand as it can be. The article below is completely neutral; it's neither anti-republican nor democrat.

Charlie Reese, a retired reporter for the Orlando Sentinel, has hit the nail directly on the head, defining clearly who it is that in the final analysis must assume responsibility for the judgments made that impact each one of us every day. It's a short but good read, worth the time and worth remembering.

545 vs. 300,000,000 People

By Charlie Reese

Politicians are the only people in the world who create problems and then campaign against them. Have you ever wondered, if all the politicians are against deficits, WHY do we have deficits? Have you ever wondered, if all the politicians are against inflation and high taxes, WHY do we have inflation and high taxes?

- You and I don't propose a federal budget, the President does.
- You and I don't have the Constitutional authority to vote on appropriations. The House of Representatives does.
- You and I don't write the tax code, Congress does.
- You and I don't set fiscal policy, Congress does.
- You and I don't control monetary policy, the Federal Reserve Bank does.
- One hundred senators, 435 congressmen, one President, and nine Supreme Court justices equates to 545 human beings out of the 300 million are directly, legally, morally and individually responsible for the domestic problems that plague this country.

I excluded the members of the Federal Reserve Bank because that problem was created by the Congress in 1913. Congress delegated its Constitutional duty to provide sound currency to a federally chartered, but private central bank.

I excluded all the special interests and lobbyist for a sound reason. They have no legal authority. They have no ability to coerce a senator, a congressman or a President to do one cotton-picking thing. I don't care if they offer a politician $1 million dollars in cash.

The politician has the power to accept or reject it. No matter what the lobbyist promises, it is the legislator's responsibility to determine how he votes.

Those 545 human beings spend much of their energy convincing you that what they did is not their fault. They cooperate in this common con regardless of party.

What separates a politician from a normal human being is an excessive amount of gall. No normal human being would have the gall of a Speaker, who stood up and criticized the President for creating deficits. The President can only propose a budget, he cannot force the Congress to accept it.

The constitution, which is the supreme law of the land, gives sole responsibility to the House of Representatives for originating and approving appropriations and taxes. Who is the speaker of the House now? He is the leader of the majority party. He and fellow House members, not the President, can approve any budget they want. If the President vetoes it, they can pass it over his veto if they agree to.

It seems inconceivable to me that a nation of 300 million cannot replace 545 people who stand convicted—by present facts—of incompetence and irresponsibility. I can't think of a single domestic problem that is not traceable directly to those 545 people.

When you fully grasp the plain truth that 545 people exercise the power of the federal government, then it must follow that what exists is what they want to exist.

- If the tax code is unfair, it's because they want it unfair.
- If the budget is in the red, it's because they want it in the red.
- If the Army and Marines are in Iraq and Afghanistan, it's because they want them in Iraq and Afghanistan.
- If they do not receive Social Security but are on an elite retirement plan not available to the people, it's because they want it that way.
- There are no insoluble government problems.

Do not let these 545 people shift the blame to bureaucrats, whom they hire and whose jobs they can abolish; to lobbyists, whose gifts and advice they can reject; to regulators, to whom they give the power to regulate and from whom they can take this power.

Above all, do not let them con you into the belief that there exists disembodied mystical forces like "the economy," "inflation," or "politics" that prevent them from doing what they take an oath to do.

Those 545 people and they alone, are responsible. They and they alone, have the power. They and they alone, should be held accountable by the people who are their bosses. Provided the voters have the gumption to manage their own employees.

We should vote all of them out of office and clean up their mess.

Charlie Reese is a former columnist of the Orlando Sentinel Newspaper.

A poem about taxes:

Tax his land,
Tax his bed,
Tax the table,
At which he's fed.

Tax his tractor,
Tax his mule,
Teach him taxes,
Are the rule.

Tax his work,
Tax his pay,
He works for,
Peanuts anyway.

Tax his cow,
Tax his goat,
Tax his pants,
Tax his coat.

Tax his ties,
Tax his shirt,
Tax his work,
Tax his dirt.

Tax his tobacco,
Tax his drink,
Tax him if he,
Tries to think.

Tax his cigars,
Tax his beers,
If he cries,
Tax his tears.

Tax his car,
Tax his gas,
Find other ways,
To tax his ***.

Tax all he has,
Then let him know,
That you won't be done,
Til he has no dough.

When he screams and hollers,
Then tax him some more,
Tax him till,
He's good and sore.

Then tax his coffin,
Tax his grave,
Tax the sod in,
Which he's laid.

Put these words,

Upon his tomb,
Taxes drove me,
To my doom.

When he's gone,
Do not relax,
It's time to apply,
The inheritance tax.

Then there is the:
Accounts receivable tax
- Building Permit tax
- CDL license tax
- Cigarette tax
- Corporate income tax
- Dog license tax
- Excise tax
- Federal income tax
- Federal unemployment tax (FUTA)
- Fishing license tax
- Food license tax
- Fuel permit tax
- Gasoline tax (currently 44.75 cents per gallon)
- Gross receipts tax
- Hunting license tax
- Inheritance tax
- Inventory tax
- IRS interest charges
- IRS penalties (tax upon tax)
- Liquor tax
- Luxury taxes
- Marriage license tax
- Medicare tax
- Personal property tax
- Property tax
- Real estate tax
- Service charge tax
- Social Security tax
- Road usage tax
- Recreational vehicle tax
- Sales tax
- School tax
- State income tax
- State unemployment tax (SUTA)

- Telephone Federal excise tax
- Telephone Federal Universal Service Fee Tax
- Telephone Federal, State and Local Surcharge Tax
- Telephone Minimum Usage Surcharge Tax
- Telephone recurring and Non-Recurring Charges Tax
- Telephone State and Local Tax
- Telephone Usage Charge Tax
- Utility Taxes
- Vehicle License Registration Tax
- Vehicle Sales Tax
- Watercraft Registration Tax
- Well Permit Tax
- Workers compensation Tax

A bit overwhelming when it's spelled out isn't it?

Not one of these taxes existed 100 years ago, and our nation was the most prosperous in the world. We had absolutely no national debt, had the largest middle class in the world, and Mom, if agreed, stayed home to raise the kids.

What in the heck happened? (Can you spell politicians?)

HOW LONG DOES THE USA HAVE

About The time our original thirteen states adopted their new constitution in 1787, Alexander Tyler, a Scottish history professor at the University of Edinburgh, had this to say about the fall of the Athenian Republic some 2,000 years earlier:

"A democracy will continue to exist up until the time that voters discover they can vote themselves generous gifts from the public treasury."

"From that moment on, the majority always vote for the candidates who promise the most benefits from the public treasury, with the result that every democracy will finally collapse due to loose fiscal policy, which is always followed by a dictatorship."

"The average age of the world's greatest civilizations from the beginning of history, has been about 200 years. During those 200 years, those nations always progressed through the following sequence:"

1. From bondage to spiritual faith;

2. From spiritual faith to great courage;
3. From courage to liberty;
4. From liberty to abundance;
5. From abundance to complacency;
6. From complacency to apathy;
7. From apathy to dependence;
8. From dependence back into bondage'

Professor Joseph Olson of Hemline University School of Law, Saint Paul, Minnesota, points out some interesting facts concerning the 2000 Presidential election:

1. Number of States won by:
2. Gore: 19
3. Bush: 29
4. Square miles of land won by:
5. Gore: 580
6. Bush: 2,427,000
7. Population of Counties won by:
8. Gore: 127 million
9. Bush: 143 million
10.   Murder rate per 100,000 residents in counties won by:
11.   Gore: 13.2
12.   Bush: 2.1

Professor Olson adds: "in aggregate, the map of the territory Bush won was mostly the land owned by the taxpaying citizens of this great country"

"Gore's territory mostly encompassed those citizens living in government-owned tenements and living off various forms of government welfare". Olson believes the United States is now somewhere between the 'complacency and apathy' phase of Professor Tyler's definition of democracy, with some forty percent of the nation's population already having reached the 'governmental dependency' phase.

If Congress grants amnesty and citizenship to twenty million criminal invaders called illegals and they get to vote, then we can say goodbye to the USA in fewer than five years.

Please pass along a special thank you to Al Gore for "inventing" the Internet, without which I would not have had all these wonderful stories to put into my little book.

CHAPTER IV The Psychosomatic Mind

Some people like to call the psychosomatic mind, the reactive mind or sub-conscious mind. Sub meaning 'below', con meaning 'with' and 'scious' meaning awareness or understanding. To me this breaks down as the mind that you cannot easily access by yourself as it is 'below your awareness', (however you can access it with help if you know how).

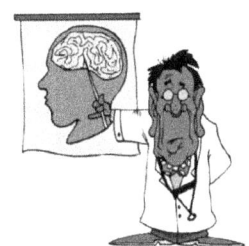

On the other hand, your conscious mind breaks down to 'the mind that you are aware of and that you can access', (con-scious/with-awareness).

For purposes of saving me some typing time, I will refer to the two minds as reactive and conscious.

In my past studies, I have been told that the reactive mind was created to keep you from making the same disastrous mistakes in life over and over again.

If you get hit by a car at night and the headlights are shining in your face while you are laying there in pain and unconscious or nearly unconscious and fearing for your life, your reactive mind will begin recording the event with or without your consent. This recording is supposed to serve you during the next time you are faced with a similar incident, (lights in your eyes) and by design, should you be faced with another bright light shining in your face, your reactive mind memories may force you to run for your life to keep you from being 'run over' again.

This would be great except for one problem. The reactive mind only sees 'similarities' and not 'similarities and differences'. So, if someone shines a flashlight in your face while hiking on a mountain slope and your reactive mind sees it as another car coming at you and makes you jump for your life, depending on the direction you jump, you may get into deep trouble. It works much like being hypnotized.

Your reactive mind has millions of recorded calculations stored just waiting to pop to the surface.

Sit down and make a list of all the things or situations that really bother you and you may get an idea of how many incidents may be on the surface of your reactive mind.

As I said before, the incident could have been recorded in your reactive mind a long, long time ago. Your reactive mind doesn't seem to care how long ago the incident occurred, and if you cause it to come to the surface by creating a similar incident, it will have an effect upon you whether you believe in it or not.

I have had approximately 800 hours of regression processing into my reactive memories. Once you recall an incident and look at it thoroughly, the 'spell', (so to speak) is lessoned. I have recalled several reactive mind incidents during my many hours of regression.

At the age of 14, I wanted to learn how to play golf. I had my own money that I earned on the weekends so I signed up for golf lessons. When the day came to go out on a course and play an actual game, I took my hat, and glove and rented some shoes and clubs. Everything was going about as good as my instructor expected for about 3 holes, and then I became nauseous. This was accompanied with a blurry, stinging sensation in my eyes, a plugged nose and a sore throat. The symptoms increased in severity and we had to stop playing for the day.

I tried several times later on to play, but the same thing happened each time. I went to our family Doctor and took a battery of tests to see if I had allergies, but all the tests came back negative. I was finally forced to give up the idea of playing golf. During my middle thirties, I met a fellow Engineer while working as an Engineer on the Apollo Spacecraft program. We met during lunch while playing in a chess tournament at work.

We talked about our various hobbies, likes and dislikes and I told him about the golfing incident. He told me about an organization that could help me discover if my subconscious mind was reacting to something out on the golf course. He took me to one of the meetings and I was hooked.

After a few weeks of studying and searching through my reactive mind I found the answer. The following seems a bit bizarre, however, it is true.

When my Mother was pregnant with me and I was about 8 months along, she got angry with my Father and was going to drive off in the family car. This was the year of 1932, in South Sioux City, Nebraska, and our car did not have an electric starter.

Mother stuck the crank into the engine and started to crank the car. The engine backfired and spun the crank back around in the opposite direction hitting Mother in the stomach and breaking my nose. Mother went immediately into pain and screamed for my Dad. Dad started the car and off we went to the Sioux City, Iowa 4th Street Hospital.

The Doctor thought I was dead, and back in 1932 the stethoscope was about the only means he had for proving otherwise. My Mother was screaming like a banshee, and the Doctor couldn't hear my heartbeat, so thinking I was dying he decided to force my birth. I hadn't turned yet and was upside down to a normal birth, so somehow the Doctor turned me: (more screaming like a banshee).

After the Doctor got me turned he hit another problem, my shoulders were too wide and all he could get out was my head, (by this time my Mother had passed out cold) so he placed a metal clamp, with a handle on it, around the top of my head clamping at my forehead and the back of my head. He took hold of the handle and began pulling.

After he got me out, he laid me on a table, <u>flat on my back</u>, (remember this for later) and began digging at my nose to get all the blood out so I could breathe better.

After that, he put drops in my eyes that made them sting, and swabbed my throat until it was as dry as sand.

The person who was helping me find all this data had me go over and over it, and after about the 10th time, a light went on and I figured out that these symptoms were exactly the same as the symptoms I had when I went out on the golf course, and with a bang-it came to me.

Putting the golfing hat on my head was so similar to the clamp the Doctor used at my birth, my reactive mind was trying to force me to take off the hat, (clamp), by running the same symptoms on me.

Later on I recalled that during a school play in the 7th grade, (we were putting on a show about American Indians), and when the teacher placed the feathered band around my head, I forgot all my lines and nearly passed out.

After running several more similar incidents, I discovered wearing a hat no longer affected me and I was able to go back to golfing without all the symptoms turning on again. .

I was never one to stand back and be shy about meeting and talking to new acquaintances, and when I found out my neighbor 3 doors down liked to play horseshoes, it wasn't too long that I had him over to my house playing the game in my back yard. We became very good friends and the games became semi-serious.

One time during a game, our horseshoes were lying at almost an equal distance from the post and I started to reach for mine saying, "I won that toss". Just as

I was bending over to pick up my horseshoe, he held my head down and playfully slapped me on the small of my back to show his disagreement.

I immediately went to my knees in pain and couldn't stand up. My L4 and L5 discs had ruptured. Remembering the birth episode, I called a friend of mine who was skilled in handling the reactive mind and we sat down, (I couldn't stand anyway) and we started looking, (regressing back into my past).

My Father died just before my 4th birthday, and up until I went to live with my Maternal Grandmother, I stayed with my Step-Grandfather, He was very mean and made me sit in the middle of his living room floor with my toys and wouldn't let me get up and run around. I was not the nicest little kid in the neighborhood, and when angered I would defend myself by kicking people in the shins.

It seems I kicked this Grandfather one time too many and one day he caught me by the back of my neck, bent me over and hit me in the small of my back with his cane. Eureka, there went L4 and L5. My back hurt for a long time, and he told me, that if I told my Mother, he would hit me harder the next time, so I kept it to myself and totally put it out of my mind until the day of the horseshoe incident.

Finding this incident relieved me of the back pain from my friend slapping my back, however I have yet to totally handle the back incident and because there was actual physical damage done when I was young, I am still bothered from time to time with back pains, (like twisting while doing some heavy 'stupid' lifting).

Another incident I discovered came from a time when I was four years old. Because I had a very bad habit of eating all the candy I could get my hands on, I was blessed with tooth cavities at the young age of four years old. One day my Mother literally dragged me to the town dentist. I was screaming and kicking all the way.

The entrance to the office was at the end of a long flight of stairs. At the top of the stairs was a small area, dimly lighted with a couple hard, wooden chairs. Since this dentist was known as a children's dentist, there were a few toys in a wooden box sitting on the floor in the corner. When the dentist took me into his room of torture, he told my Mother to stay behind in the waiting room.

Being 1936, the dentist only had laughing gas and chloroform to deaden the pain while he dug away at my tooth. He elected to use chloroform on me and this brought about my first out of body experience.

As he was working on pulling my tooth, I left my body and went to try and get my Mother to help save me from this monster. When I finally found my way to my Mother, she was playing with a little girl that was waiting for her turn in the torture chamber. I couldn't understand why my Mother wouldn't pay any attention to me. I was screaming at her to save me, but she just ignored me and kept on playing with the girl.

At that moment I decided I hated girls and from that day forward they would rue the day they kept my Mother from helping me.

After several attempts to get my Mothers attention, I went back into my body and decided then and there that no one would ever be able to put me unconscious again. (Doctors today marvel at how much anesthesia it takes to put me under).

After the Dentist finished with my tooth, he laid me on my back on a wooden bench and after he turned his back to me to walk away, I promptly rolled off the bench, fell face down on the floor and broke my nose again.

Oh, My Lord, how I hate dentists. To all the little girls whose lives I made a living hell because of this incident, I deeply apologize and hope I did not cause you to have a long lasting hatred of little boys.

After I discovered what happened, the next time I saw my Mother I told her of the information I pulled from the incidents, and her mouth dropped open and she demanded to know who told me, as she wanted all of the negative incidents to be kept secret from me.

My Mother was the kind of person who could take harmful or negative information to her grave and never speak of it if she thought for one second it could harm someone. She was an absolute Saint. She was sometimes misguided, but nevertheless a Saint.

The following statement may seem to be straying away from the subject of the psychosomatic mind, but I assure you, if you stay with me on this you will see the connection.

I'm going to ask for your indulgence while I stray into the twilight zone for a minute. I would like to paint a 'what if' scenario for you. If past lives were an absolute fact, let us take a look and see what 'might' come from them.

This is a theory that I came up with and I could be way off base but what the heck. Let's say that a young girl reaches her teen years and has discussed, (having sex, getting married, having children, a Husband and a home), with some of her schoolmates.

Then like the many young girls here in the United States that were kidnapped and later found murdered, she was kidnapped and killed. She will probably go to the 'LIGHT' still carrying all the desires and hopes of being a grown woman with all the perks that go with it.

Let us then assume she comes back into another life and is born a girl again. All those desires from her last lifetime are under the surface of her awareness, but they are there just the same. This time she possibly grows to a ripe old age of 20, before she 'pulls in' another murderer to do her in. Now she has compounded all the desires from her last life and this life, 'to grow up and become a complete woman'.

She now has two lifetimes of incomplete female desires clinging to her. The next time she comes back down to Earth to begin another life, it is possible that she could be born into a male body. What do you think will happen to 'him' if all the earlier 'female' desires get accidentally brought to the surface of his/her reactive mind ? She, (the spirit) will be a person with strong desires to be a woman and have the things a woman would have, but 'she' will be in a male body. This theory works in regards to young boys who may get reborn in a female body also.

In California, we have kidnappings or attempted kidnappings of young girls all too often. For myself, I know past lives exist, and for me this theory is not a far stretch of my imagination. I for one would be totally uncomfortable in a female body, and believe it or not, I actually left a female baby body when I found out I wasn't born into a male body. The Coroner called it 'crib death'. But, that's a 'bizarre' story for another time.

I hope I have given you a little insight into the reactive mind and how it functions. I have looked at hundreds of my reactive mind incidents and I would enjoy relating them all to you. Perhaps I will do a past life book and put them all in.

Many people that have had mental problems in the past have been subjected to electro-shock therapy. In my opinion the electro-shock doesn't cure anyone, it merely keeps the unwanted memories from coming to the surface and being accessed.

I've been told that the electro-shock also scatters, (shuffles around) the chronological order of many of the past and present time life incidents making it almost impossible to do regression therapy afterwards.

To those people who don't believe in past lives, incidents or regression therapy, if I were in your place, I still would never subject myself to electro-shock therapy.

CHAPTER V Illnesses, a few tips

In this chapter I want to bring the reactive mind back into the conversation. I used to get a cold and/or influenza at least once a year. The class supervisor, (at the organization I was attending learning how to regress back and handle past incidents) said to me, "as you go up the scale toward a higher level of knowledge and awareness, the colds will go away".

During the coffee break chats with fellow students, we discussed how one must learn how to 'stay in present time' at all times in order to keep well and avoid 'turning on' the reactive mind. Well fine, but how in the heck do you 'stay in present time'?

The closest I could come to it on my own was to try and 'be totally aware of what was going on around me at all times'. However, I discovered that wasn't enough. There were other factors involved.

Those factors are: **Losses and the reactive mind.** Did I say losses? Yes, I said losses. I had double trouble with mine. Every time I met someone who was similar, (in any way) to someone I had lost from my past, I would start to come down sick with either a cold or the Flu.

After a while, if I felt a cold coming on, I discovered that if I could find a quiet corner and sit down and meditate on who it may have been that triggered my reactive mind, sometimes I could discover who the person I met reminded me of and the cold or Flu would go away on the spot.

This was a form of being reminded of someone who was lost or gone from me. If you lose your spouse, a family member, or a long time family pet you could develop a major illness.

Maybe you lost out on doing something because you couldn't pass a test or your parents wouldn't allow you to go somewhere you had your heart set on going. These are losses that cause illnesses. When my two Daughters had to go back to school and lost their summer vacation, they would get a cold. Then, when school was over and they were going into their summer vacation, they would get a cold again. Why? When they left school, they were 'losing' all their friends, and when they went back to school, they were 'losing' all their fun and free time.

I really get a 'kick' out of people that tell me they caught a cold because they left their bedroom window open. I am a 'cover kicker' and my Wife left our bedroom window open all the time. I woke up every morning freezing with no covers on me and the window still open and 'I didn't get colds because of it'. Our bodies were designed to withstand heat and cold. If you are totally exhausted and haven't taken care of yourself, I can understand why you are getting sick. Your body was half way there already.

If you ask most doctors, "what causes colds and Flu", they usually say, "it is because your resistance went down". OK, so ask them, "gee doc, what makes my resistance go down"? One answer he won't give you is: 'losses'. If you start to come down with a cold or Flu, go off somewhere by yourself where you won't be disturbed and ask yourself, "In the past three days, who or what is gone".

Or perhaps ask "within the past three days, who or what have I lost"? The reason for the 'in the past three days' pre-empt is because you could accidentally go back into a past lifetime looking for something you lost. Yes, I said Past Lifetime. I warned you this reading may get a little bizarre at times.

When I was young, (this lifetime) I collected pocket watches, pocketknives and harmonicas. I never made much of it, but my parents accused me of driving them crazy with my hobby. I went to every antique dealer I could find every time my parents took me along on a trip. I taught myself how to play the harmonica at the age of five. And I mean PLAY the harmonica, not just blow into it.

Every day in grade school, several of us kids traded pocketknives 'sight unseen' with the school crossing guard. In the fifth grade, I traded a pocketknife with the school crossing guard and received in return a yellow handled, small, two bladed, pocketknife, and I unconsciously said, "this is the one". I never traded that knife away and today at eighty two years old, I still have that knife. I have my Father's pocket watch that my Mother bought for him in 1928. I had it completely restored in 1982 and put it away for safe keeping. Why all this collecting? Let me tell you the story. Remember, we are discussing losses....

This incident happened during one of my past lives, during a war, (similar to the civil war between the North and the South). I was a Captain and in charge of several cannons. We were involved in a long drawn out battle. The enemy was taking cover in a stand of trees on the other side of a large field in front of us. All of our cannons were lined up facing the stand of trees on the opposite side of the field. When the enemy soldiers attacked again, my plan was to let them advance until they were in range of our cannons and then I would signal the crew of cannon number one to fire. When cannon number one fired, it was to be the signal for all the other cannons to fire.

We had just driven the enemy back into the trees with a volley of cannon and rifle fire from our riflemen in our trenches and soldiers manning our cannons were busy reloading. Perhaps some of you are not aware of how dangerous the old black powder cannons were out on a field of battle. Some of them blew apart after a few rounds were fired through them, taking the lives of anyone standing within a few feet.

After the cannons were fired, the soldier loading each cannon is required to stoke and reload the cannon, (put out the remaining powder bag's burning embers or force the burning embers out through the touch hole). He did this by ramming a broom handle like pole, (having wet rags wrapped around the end) down the barrel of the cannon until he was fairly certain he had extinguished all the burning embers. He then would ram, (with the same pole) two or three bags of black gunpowder down the barrel, followed by the ball or shot. If he hurried the job and didn't get all the embers extinguished, it was possible for those remaining hot embers to prematurely ignite the bags of powder and fire his cannon blowing the ramming pole or the ball out of the cannon before we were ready.

That is what happened to me while I was standing 10 or 15 feet out in front of cannon number 2 looking through my binoculars. The number 2 cannon went off while I was standing out in front of the line and the ball took half my face and jaw off. When the cannon went off, all the others took it as the signal to fire and a full volley of cannon balls were wasted on an empty field. The enemy was confused for a few moments, but then realized what had happened and charged our line.

Instead of reloading, the men at the cannons ran and left our riflemen in the trenches to fend for themselves. We lost that battle in only a few minutes, and after the smoke cleared and everyone moved on, a couple of renegade soldiers, (we called them scavengers) came through the battle field looking for gold teeth, money, hand guns, and anything else of value, such as **'harmonicas, pocketknives and pocket watches'**. Yes, the two scavengers picked my pockets and took my treasures. I was still alive, but that didn't stop them from taking a rifle butt and breaking the rest of my face open and prying out my gold teeth. Fortunately when they hit me with the rifle butt, they knocked me unconscious again. There I was, **lying on my back** with my **nose broken**, unconscious with pain and a definite threat to my survival and, my 'reactive mind recording'.

115

This incident set me on a quest in all of my next lifetimes, to find my lost treasures. After many hour of regression in this lifetime, I was finally able to put the need to collect pocket knives, harmonicas and pocket watches behind me. The strange thing about all that is, during all my studies of the reactive mind, I had a hard time being convinced that it was possible for the reactive mind to record sights, sounds and the other senses while being unconscious. After a few hundred hours of reviewing many incidents over many past lives, I became convinced that it was not only definitely possible, but for me became a reality.

It is a very simple process to view the incidents stored within your reactive mind. The trick is to be able to make the connection between the present day problems and phobias you have and how the incident stored in your reactive mind created the problems or phobias. Some people can view the incident once and immediately see the connection. Others may have to view the incident several times before making the connection. After viewing more and more incidents, you become more able to 'stay in present time'.

After a while people you meet will no longer remind you of your losses nor turn on your reactive mind, and you will find you are not getting sick as often. You will be in present time and if you lose something, you will immediately cancel the illness by being aware of the loss. How many of you saw the movie, "You have mail"?

When Tom Hanks caused Meg Ryan to lose her bookstore, she became ill within a couple days. Isn't it strange how screenplay writers 'unconsciously' write in an illness after a loss!

Headaches can come about in a similar manner. My Wife had migraine headaches from the time she started Kindergarten school. I have always been two steps off the beaten trail when it comes to having a standard medical doctor, and my choice of healing at the time my Wife and I married was Chinese acupuncture.

I talked my Wife into going to my acupuncturist for treatment. He treated her for about 3 months, and then one day after her treatment, he said, "ok, go home now, no come back, no more headaches".

For the rest of her life, she never suffered from another migraine headache. Since then, I have found a second way to handle 'some' headaches. I'm not professing to be a medical diagnostician, nor am I attempting to perform any medical procedures. I do know a form of meditation that makes my headaches go away, and I would like to pass it on to you. If it works for you, great!

Here it is: When you feel a headache pain coming on, take one of your fingers, and touch the spot where the pain is emanating. Close your eyes and do your best to really feel the pain. Turn the pain on as strong as you can. After you have turned the pain on as strong as you can, then take your finger away and stop trying to feel the pain.

Close your eyes and go off into your memories, find a time when you were really happy and having a good time. A favorite place where you enjoyed being. Keep your eyes closed and "Look around and tell yourself what you see there" then, "Listen and tell yourself what you hear there" then, "Smell and tell yourself what you smell there" then, "Feel and tell yourself what you feel there" then "Taste and tell yourself what you taste there".

If by this time the pain has not vanished, then return your finger to the place where the pain is emanating and turn the pain on as strongly as you can again. Alternate between doing the above actions, putting your finger at the point of the pain and feeling the pain and then going off into your memories, finding a time and place when you were very happy and ask yourself the questions again. Continue the above actions until you cannot feel the pain or until the pain diminishes enough that you can live with it.

Most people only require 3 or 4 'trips' to a happy place and the pain goes away. You can choose a different 'Happy place' or return to the same one until you have exhausted all of the sights, sounds and all the other senses at that place. As an example, the beach has many things to see, smell, hear, touch and taste if you allow yourself the time to re-experience them.

You can do this action for others also. Just have them put their finger on their spot of pain and give them the commands instead of giving them to yourself.

When you are helping another you need to say 'thank you' or 'alright' or 'good', each time they give you an answer. Without this they will think you are not really listening and will eventually stop responding to your commands.

One of the causes for headaches I have found in my case is 'should haves' and 'shouldn't haves'. Sounds silly, I know, but it really works. If you do something you know you shouldn't have done, or if you don't do something you know you should have done, (and you have a conscience), you may pull a headache in on yourself. This all goes back to the statement, 'stay in present time'. Be aware of what is happening to you and be aware of and stop doing the non-survival acts you are doing to, and saying about, others and 'yourself' and you may have fewer headaches and more friends.

I have just lately been made aware of something that you may be interested in. If you have ever owned a swimming pool, you are well aware of the work it requires to keep the PH factor of the water 'neutral'. If pool water becomes very acidic, almost anything bad can grow on the surfaces of the pool itself and in and on the water.

It seems, (I've been told) that our bodies have the same PH problem also. There exists a small green and white book called 'Home Test PH Kit' that you really need to purchase and read. It was written by Deborah Page Johnson, BFA. I found it to be extremely informative and interesting. It explains the whole PH subject and you will enjoy it completely. Your body's PH can be acidic, neutral or alkaline.

When you buy the book, make sure you get the litmus paper with it. The paper will test your PH for you and when you do, you will be amazed. If your body PH is very acidic, any unwanted tumors, cists, warts or whatever can exist in and on your body.

There are machines available through the internet that you can pour bottled water into and the machine will turn the water 'alkaline'. You drink the alkaline water and eventually your body will reach a neutral PH. You use the litmus paper to monitor your PH and drink accordingly.

A Man my youngest Daughter knows told my Daughter about this. It seems my Daughter's friend has a Sister-in-law who had pancreatic cancer and during the attempted surgery the doctors sewed her back together and told her later that there was nothing they could do for her. They told her she had 3 months to live.

Her Brother-in law bought an alkaline machine and started her drinking large amounts and lo and behold she is now several years older and cancer free.

We just brought our eldest Daughter home from the hospital with a large tumor in the airway to her right lung. Her right lung has collapsed.

We are getting a machine and starting her on the alkaline water next week. I'll let you know what happens in my next book.

CHAPTER VI
One of the Causes of High School Drop Outs

How many times during school hours did you sit and stare out of the classroom window and watch the birds peck in the grass? It was several times for me. I was a High School dropout. Some of the subjects were just too 'tough' for me. Like: English, Math, History, Spanish, PE, Biology, Auto Shop, Wood Shop and Lunch.

I wish I would have known then what I know now. There is a definite reason for being able to pay attention and retain knowledge, versus staring out the window. Would you believe it was because you passed a **word or symbol** that you didn't fully understand? That's right, the teacher spoke a word or several words that you did not understand, and you just turned off.

The same thing can happen while you are reading. It just drives me crazy to see school kids involved in deep study, reading, and learning and **passing over words** they clearly do not understand.

I had an employee that ran a machine for me several years ago. He wanted to better himself and decided he would go back to school. He went to one of the vocational schools that teach just what you need to enter a vocation of your choice. After two weeks, he came to me and said he was going to quit school.

When I asked why, he said, "I just can't learn the math". I told him to bring his math book into work the next day. When he brought me the book, I asked him what page he was on and I think he said something like page forty two. I scanned through pages one through ten and picked out a large word that I figured he didn't know.

I asked him, "What does this word mean to you"? He didn't know. I chose a couple more words on the next page with the same results, he didn't know them either. After showing him several words he couldn't define, I then asked him "How in the h___ did you get on page forty two, when you couldn't get past page ten"?

He got the point right away and wanted to know what he was doing wrong. I told him he needed to carry a dictionary around with him 24/7. That means all day, every day during his study time.

Don't buy a huge collegiate type dictionary. Get an 8th grade dictionary (like the American Heritage dictionary) that will give you definitions you can understand without ending up having more words to look up. At the end of two more weeks, he was doing great and enjoying every minute of his class. He is now a successful architect with a home larger than mine. True Story.

How do you know if you have skipped over a word you didn't understand? The first indication you will notice, is, you will 'yawn'. If you are reading a book and you start yawning, you need to look back and scan the paragraph you just read and if you don't remember the data in the paragraph, and yet you know you read it, look back before that paragraph and find where you last remember what you read and then scan forward to where you lost it, and somewhere sitting there in-between the two areas, you will find a word or words that you skipped over and it/they turned you off like a turning off a 'LIGHT'.

If you have children in school and they are having study problems, pick up one of their books and starting about twenty pages ahead of where they are in the book, look for words they may have skipped over, and for each word you find, ask them, "what does this word mean to you"? I think you will be amazed by how many words they have skipped over with no concept whatsoever of their meaning.

If they have been skipping past words for quite a while it may take some time for them to catch up and learn how to stay in present time while studying. When a student skips over many words over a great length of time, he or she begins to feel stupid and gives up trying to learn what ever subject they are having problems with.

However, if you can convince them to go back and clear up all the words they skipped over and keep trying to stay in present time and not skip over any more words, you will see them change very quickly and hopefully become an "A" student very soon. Most kids have problems with learning Algebra.

If you have a child who doesn't quite believe all this and they are having a problem with Algebra, and you want to make a point about all this, tell them that you know the very first word they skipped over in their algebra class. When they challenge your power of awareness, just ask them "What is the dictionary definition of the word Algebra"? I can almost guarantee that they won't know it. POINT MADE!

I have written a seven page letter to our California Governor on this subject, hoping he would try an experiment in our California elementary schools using it. But, since he has spent so much time as an actor, and actors love being interesting, He apparently is too busy being "interesting" and not being "interested".

If it was just a matter of his letter screener not thinking the data was worth bothering him with, then he has my retraction and my apology. I can tell you this, I told him in the same letter that I thought he should do away with the double yellow lines that separate the car pool lane from the regular lanes on our Southern California Freeways. This would allow people to go in and out of the car pool lane at any point on the freeway. For me at my age, it is very difficult to exit the car pool lane in the short distance allowed in heavy traffic.

Many times I have missed my off ramp due to heavy 'California crazy' traffic. My argument to our Governor was that Highways 50 and 80 in Northern California have never, (to my knowledge) had double yellow lines separating the car pool lane from the other lanes.

Two months after my letter – our Governor came out with the statement that he was going to re-do our Southern California freeway #22 and would try an experiment by not putting double yellow lines between the car pool lane and the other lanes.

The newly reworked 215 freeway North of the 60 freeway has been changed to double white lines on the diamond lane also. Gosh, I wonder where he got that idea if he indeed did not get my letter. Oh well, I guess I expect way too much from our politicians.

The Honorable Ken Calvert:

My friend Pete and I went to a town meeting to see our Honorable congressman for our Riverside district. I had several subjects I wanted to bring to his attention but he couldn't get past the fact that I was in the NRA and AOPA. I don't want to leave you with an unknown symbol so AOPA stands for the Aircraft Owners and Pilots Association and just about everyone knows that the NRA stands for the National Rifleman's Association. As I was saying, my good friend Pete and I went to the meeting and sat down in chairs near at the end of the row next to the exit.

Our congressman came over to us first and introduced himself to us. My Granddaughter had been in several parades in Corona, California in which our congressman had ridden on a float several times and when he shook my hand I reminded him that I was the guy who stood on the sidewalk at the parades he was in and that I was shouting NRA-AOPA. He jerked his hand away from mine and very rudely said, **"Yeah, I know- lock up criminals not guns".**

The main reason I had gone to see him was in behalf of two very good friends of mine who were in the same type of electronic assembly business as I. They were $20,000 in debt to the IRS, (thanks to a cheating employee) and making payments to the IRS as best they could.

The IRS was threatening to take their house away from them and over time had increased their debt to $80,000.00. That is when I stepped in and went to talk to the **Honorable** Riverside congressman.

Well, I kept my hand raised the total time of the meeting, but our congressman probably thinking I was there to complain about the new laws against the NRA, would not call upon me. Another person was there for the same IRS complaint and while she was explaining her plight, I chided in about how my friends were being treated also.

By this time I was so angry I got up and walked out with Pete following me. After the IRS debt reached $80,000 my friend Marylou died from the stress and her Husband disappeared never to be seen by me again. I did have an opportunity to discuss the 'skipping past words' with our congressman and he told me, "That is a State problem and has nothing to do with National".

I held my anger in right up until the tax time of 2006 when my tax attorney told me, "Ed, your congressman didn't have the power to help your friends with the IRS problem in the first place. All of congress promised a couple years ago to reform the IRS and it hasn't happened and it never will.

I personally feel he is a minor congressman who promises much and achieves very little". So, congressman, I have put all the anger toward you behind me, but I still think you are small minded and I don't like you very much at all.

Ironically I first met our congressman when he came to an NRA meeting when he first ran for office and told all of us at the meeting that he would be a strong supporter of the NRA. He was all smiles and handshakes **then.** I think Ken is descended from the politicians that drew up the treaties with our American Indians.

CHAPTER VII Do 'UFO's' really exist?

I haven't seen a UFO yet. And I stress the word 'yet'. I have two four foot long shelves in my office with almost every flying saucer report put into a magazine or newspaper back in 1965. I was a great follower of Major Donald Keyhoe. He was the founder of NICAP, (The National Investigating Committee on Aerial Phenomena).

I was asked to chair the Los Angeles Committee of NICAP, but I was working as an Engineer on the Apollo Spacecraft project at the time and I was being a Husband to my Wife, a Father to my two Daughters and had very little free time at all so I had to decline.

I had a newspaper clipping service and I bought every magazine that had a UFO story in it, and fortunately we were in the middle of a UFO 'flap', (a period in 1965 where several UFO's were sighted every day).

One day the Orange County Register newspaper came out with pictures of a UFO that an Orange County government employee had taken in Orange County, California. I contacted the man and asked him for an interview. His name was Rex Heflin. One of my co-workers and I went to his house with a tape recorder and taped his story. He was a county employee and his job was to go into areas in the county that were possibly hazardous areas that needed county attention, (pot holes in the street, school crossings that needed stop signs, weed control, fire prevention, etc).

He carried a Polaroid camera with him everywhere he went, and during the time of our friendship, showed me pictures that he had taken of cars in midair, in collisions.

This is the story as it unfolded. Rex was in his county work truck parked facing North on Myford Road in Tustin, California and had just written up a problem with the road. He was parked at the side of the road, and was in the process of lighting a cigar, when

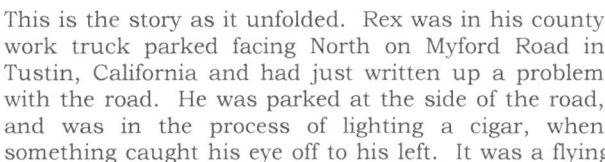

something caught his eye off to his left. It was a flying saucer wobbling a few feet off the ground over a dirt field to his front left.

He grabbed his camera and snapped a picture of it. It flew, wobbling slowly across in front of the truck and paused off to the right of him over a second dirt field. He snapped two more pictures just before it flew off down the road in front of him and crossed over the (Santa Ana 5) freeway. He fired up his truck and raced after it.

When he came out from under the freeway overpass, he saw the saucer shoot straight up into the sky and disappear. He got out of his truck with the camera and snapped a picture of a donut shaped cloud of black dust, (approximately 20 feet in diameter) that was floating down into the orange trees at the spot where the saucer had disappeared.

NICAP called one of the scientists who was working at the Jet Propulsion Laboratory here in Southern California and asked him to look into the story with us. I will refer to him as Doctor Hale. At the request of Dr. Hale, we all made arrangements to meet at the UFO site and the he also wanted copies of all the pictures of the UFO. After our meeting, he asked us to come back to the same spot on the first year anniversary of the sighting and he would have some data for us. He asked Rex to bring the same truck and the same camera if he could.

We all met on the anniversary date and Dr. Hale brought out a large white, three foot diameter model of the saucer he had created from the picture. He told Rex to park the county truck in the same spot as before and set it up exactly as it was when he took the original pictures. Rex was able to park the truck in the exact same place as before, as he found his original cigar box lying in the dirt at the side of the asphalt road where he had tossed it out of the truck window one year earlier. Dr. Hale then placed the saucer model on an adjustable pole similar to a Christmas tree stand.

He placed the saucer in several different locations and heights out in front of the truck and told Rex to take pictures, (of each position of the model) as he had one year before. After several minutes of adjusting the location of the model, while taking several pictures, he finally said, "I think we now have the right location for the model".

He was trying to get the model to appear the exact same size in the new photo as the real saucer appeared in the original photo. He explained to us that, the model only being 3 feet in diameter had to be placed closer to the truck in order for it to appear the same size as the actual saucer appeared in the original photo. He asked Rex and me if we could detect the differences between the original picture and the one Rex had just taken. We couldn't.

After some friendly razzing from Dr. Hale, he pointed out that the model was casting a shadow from the sun, onto the pavement of the road and that in the original photo there is no shadow on the pavement. He calculated that the original saucer had to be greater than 18 feet in diameter and several feet out over the plowed field in order to not cast any shadows on the pavement, (it had to be farther away and over the dirt field to not cast a shadow and therefore had to be larger to still match the size of the saucer in the original pictures).

Rex then pointed out that in the original photo there was a black shadow around the saucer covering the lower half of the windows.

Dr. Hale went to his car and brought back a round piece of foam rubber painted black and cut in the shape of the black shadow and flopped it onto the model. "Does that look like the black shadow around the windows of the saucer", he asked. He then asked, "do any of you know what it was'? None of us did. He was having great fun at our expense as he knew we were engineers and I think he was testing our ability to solve engineering problems. He finally explained what he was leading us to and it was a simple explanation.

The saucer was hovering very close to the ground and evidently as the thing traveled it created one huge magnetic field around the saucer. As it hovered close to the ground, it pulled shovels full of black iron particles from the Earth up to the area where the saucer's magnetic field was being produced, (around the bottom of the dome where the windows were).

When the saucer left Earth it changed the properties of its magnetic field and shot straight up, releasing it from the Earth and the magnetized black iron particles became de-magnetized and floated off the circular body of the saucer and back down to Earth in the shape of a large black donut.

I received a phone call from a gentleman from New Jersey. He was a narrator for several UFO shows on the History channel. Somehow he found out that I was the prime investigator on the Rex Heflin UFO sighting and wanted to know if I could make copies of all my findings. I sent him the information and a few days later he told me he had an anomaly he couldn't explain.

He said when a UFO is seen moving close to the ground either going up stream or downstream over a small stream, the water dances up in the air under the UFO. I explained that there were iron particles lying on the bottom of the stream and as the UFO passes over the stream, the iron particles are attracted to the UFO and pop water into the air as they break the surface of the stream. I didn't so much as get a thank you from him and I have written him off as a 'flake'.

The complete Rex Heflin story was documented in the book 'Flying Saucers-Serious Business' in 1966 by Frank Edwards. Some of the story that didn't make it into Frank's book was pretty humorous.

Two military men, apparently Air Force personnel, came to Rex's house one evening, flashed a long plastic strip full of identification cards, and asked if they could take some measurements and pictures of his truck, (which was parked in his driveway). He told them sure, knock yourselves out, and they proceeded to take two dozen or more pictures of his truck. At this point in the episode, he was very upset with all the harassment he had been getting from the military, so he just let them do their thing.

I asked him what was so funny about letting them take all those pictures of his truck and he said, "I think the idiots wanted pictures of the county work truck that I used when I took the saucer pictures, not my personal truck, but I wasn't going to tell them". His last words to me were "let the idiots take all the pictures of my personal truck that they want to".

I recently found a book at a local gun show that I think everyone should read. I fear it is out of print by now, but if you can find a copy it's well worth the search. The name of the book is, "The Day after ROSWELL" by COL. Phillip J. Corso, (Ret). Being an engineer, I am always interested in new inventions and I have a few inventions on my plate as I write. I was always in awe of my fellow scientists and design engineers because of all the new innovations they have created out of their brilliant thinking.

I always believed (as I was led to believe), that all the new toys, gadgets, and inventions came from our explorations in space and from our wars with other nations.

Then I read, The Day after ROSWELL.   Put your memory to a test. Think back and list all the "new" inventions that have been created in the last fifty years. I'm talking about new things that didn't fall out of prior inventions. Can you think of any? Let me list a few:

- Fiber Optics,
- Laser Beam,
- Night Vision,
- Stealth material,
- Silicon chips,
- Particle Beam Devices
- Kevlar Material.

I had believed these were the brilliant creations of our top scientists and engineers. Right up until I read "ROSWELL, The Day after". Col. Corso explains how he was in charge of having captured enemy weapons 'reverse' engineered by various companies here in the United States, (take the items apart to see what they are made of and how they work). One day his superior gave him access to several strange objects and told him to have them reverse engineered.

However, he was not to tell anyone where they came from or how he came about having them. He said in his book that the items he was put in charge of were pulled from the wreckage of the flying saucer that crashed in Roswell, New Mexico in 1947. The items I listed above were the items Col. Corso said he was given. Col. Corso gives names, dates and all the details of his handling of the items.

From my understanding our scientists and engineers haven't really come up with anything significant in over 50 years. Nearly every new innovation over the past 50 years was born out of the objects taken from the wreckage of the Roswell saucer back in 1947. Ask senior citizens, "Who invented the phonograph", most can tell you. Ask them "Who invented the light bulb", again most can tell you. However, if you ask for the names of the inventors that invented the items from the above list, all you will get is "I don't know".

If you would like to do some of your own investigating, get on the internet and look up The Enterprise Mission.com and the Apollo Hoax.com. You will be amazed at what you find there. Please don't be angry with me over what you find there, I am but a humble Engineer and a messenger of the 'LIGHT'.

I Googled the name 'NICAP.com' on the internet and was amazed that the organization that I belonged to so many years ago was still there in all its glory with a very informing web site. If you are interested in the truth about UFO's, I know of a couple websites you can surf and explore. The three I named above make a good place to start.

You might Google the name 'Edgar Mitchell' if you really want a taste of the bizarre. He was the Commander of the Apollo 14 Spacecraft mission and about three weeks prior to my typing this sentence, he came out on Television with the statement that "UFO's are real".

I haven't had the time to search out the reason for his statement coming out so late in his life, but having been with NICAP for many years, having been an investigator on a major UFO sighting and having been an Engineer for many years on the Apollo project, I tend to believe his story whether he is telling it to make money or to clear his conscience.

You will be able to read all about the major UFO sighting that I investigated back in 1965 on the NICAP website and in my next book, "The Great UFO Flap of 1965". Back then when there were several hundred sightings all occurring within a year's time we called that a 'UFO Flap'.

CHAPTER VIII
Creation, Continuation & Ending

Have you ever noticed that objects, people, nations, etc. cycle from good to bad and back again. Some extremely simple examples are:

When the aspirin first came out, it was advertised as the best medicine for pain and headaches that you could buy. Sometime later, we were told that the aspirin was bad for your stomach and caused ulcers. Then after a third, 'some time later' we were told that aspirin could prevent us from having a second stroke if we take one a day. Make up my mind-people.

Eggs were a major staple in our diets for many years then Doctors informed us that eggs were extremely high in bad cholesterol, and urged us to cut down on them or quit eating them altogether. And now if you have been watching the TV ads you have probably noticed that the advertisers have been praising the value of the egg again, saying, "We were mistaken".

Ammonia was banned back in the 1940's because too many children were getting hurt from it. We were using the ammonia at full strength and cleaning everything around the house and garage. It was banned for many years, but now we seem to be back using it again and it is hailed as the greatest cleaner on the market.

Because of all the high speed automobile accidents that were happening some years ago, the automobile manufacturers were told by congress to put an end to advertising how fast their cars were on the open highway. Everything was all about power and speed. Now, if you have paid any attention to television ads, you will see that every ad is all about speed (zoom-zoom) again.

If you know your history books you will see a similar pattern of creation, continuance and ending. It applies to things like: the rule of Ghenges Khan, the Roman Empire, the Nazi Third Reich, the grand navies of England and Spain, the Incas, the American Indians, etc. I am fully expecting many more 'endings' to occur.

I don't want to give the impression that when 'endings' come everything is lost. Like the Phoenix bird that rises out of the ashes to be reborn, whatever is going through the 'ending' cycle will find that something new will be created in its place. When it comes time for the United States to go through it's 'ending' cycle I believe something new will arise from the ashes, be it 'World Federation', 'a Dictatorship' or whatever.

Already, our government is able to monitor every mode of communication used here in the United States, and anyone sending or receiving suspicious information will be subject to investigation. This action may someday include those who question our government's decisions and laws. This reminds me of the days during the Second World War, when our government incarcerated the Japanese people who were living here in our country.

Here I go off into the bizarre again. But, if you continue reading you will see the connection with create, continue and ending. When your body gives up and you exteriorize, hopefully you will see the 'LIGHT' and travel toward it.

After you arrive at the LIGHT and meet and greet all your 'passed over' friends and relatives that are still there at the LIGHT, you may after some time passes, begin having an urge to return to Earth and join back in on all the physical fun stuff again.

How soon until you start having the urge, will probably depend upon how good or how bad your last lifetime turned out. Just as God instilled the instinct within all living things to reproduce, He put an instinct within you and I to 'come on down' and have another go at the homo-sapiens game.

Some people that believe in past lives, say that each time we live another lifetime we do better, increase our knowledge of God and become better people.

I think you should look around at the truth. Illegal drug trafficking is getting worse, prostitution, murder and rape are as rampant as ever, our educational system is failing, new viruses are being found, our government is trying to return to the days of Edgar J. Hoover and his blacklist days. Hatred and bullying is prevalent throughout all our schools, young people shooting other young people for no or little reason and wars and rumors of wars are looming everywhere.

Are we doing better or are we in our 'destruction' cycle? I would say we are in our destruction cycle. When Christopher landed at Plymouth Rock, the United States wasn't even a glint in his eye. By the year 1998 we were at the peak of our Industrial cycle but it's been a downhill run ever since.

Whereas China has begun their upward cycle toward being an Industrial Giant as we were at one time. How long China will stay at their peak is anyone's guess.

I suppose it depends on if they become a democracy in the near future or not. Our school system in the USA is currently rated 14th throughout the world. The school system in China is currently rated number 1.

CHAPTER IX
Have you been to the 'LIGHT' lately?

When I was growing up, I never gave much thought about what my Maternal Grandmother was trying to tell me about the Bible. She lived ninety percent of her adult life in a wheel chair due to an accidental fall down a flight of basement stairs back in the nineteen twenties. Being wheel chair bound, she had a lot of time to read and contemplate the Bible.

When my Father died in 1936, Grandmother was my primary caretaker as my Mother was forced to go to work to support us all. Grandmother would read to me daily from her German Bible and explain everything as she went along. She told me that in the beginning, God said, "Let there be LIGHT", and God saw the light and said it was GOOD. She believed that the Light God was actually creating was the LIGHT of Heaven.

As an Engineer, I believe God designed our bodies   so we could not see the LIGHT until we had 'passed over', or "gone to the LIGHT" as the current thought goes.

I was taught that we could not see Heaven 'the LIGHT' because we all have to take the fact that it exists totally on faith. As an engineer, I believe that much like our inability to hear a dog whistle because our ears cannot detect that audio 'frequency', we cannot see the LIGHT of Heaven because our eyes cannot detect that 'frequency' of light. Out of the many times you may have heard or read the statement made by Jesus, ("I am the LIGHT, I am TRUTH, I am the WAY, and only through ME"), how many times did you ask yourself, what light was Jesus talking about? Was he referring to the LIGHT of Heaven?

Thought of the day: The Bible tells us that God created us ALL in his image. If you believe that literally, then why don't we ALL look alike? Figure it out.

Quite a few people have claimed to have had near death experiences and traveled through a dark tunnel before seeing the LIGHT. I had a similar experience when I was involved in an explosion in 1951 at a Division of Douglas Aircraft which killed nine other employees.

My co-worker and I would place honeycomb insulation paper into metal trays and dip the trays into tanks, (the tanks were nine feet long by three feet wide and two feet deep) filled with a mixture of alcohol and varnish (long before the EPA-Environmental Protection Agency existed),

One evening, (I worked second shift), our department quality control inspector came in to measure the content of the alcohol mixture in the tank. My co-worker and I were not aware that the inspector was 'drunk as a skunk', and had placed the wrong test float probe into the tanks. After taking the reading with the wrong probe, he instructed us to pump more alcohol in the tanks. I informed him that I had just taken a measurement with our probe and had filled the tanks with the proper amount of alcohol within the past half hour. He informed me that he was the Inspector on this shift and we would do as he says (and I think he had more alcohol in his system than we had in the tank)..

So, after filling the tanks with nearly 60% too much alcohol the Inspector went 'happily' on his way. We filled ten, 10" wide by 72" long and 6" deep metal trays with honeycomb paper, dipped them in the alcohol & varnish, and placed them onto the 4 wheel "A" frame device. We then wheeled them into the 15' wide by 20' long and 10' high steel oven. We closed the 8' by 10' foot by 4" thick door and turned and walked away.

It took less than 15 seconds for the excess alcohol fumes from the paper to reach the flames of the gas heater. When the oven flames ignited the fumes from the excess alcohol, the explosive force blew me and half of the oven door 60 feet down to the other end of the building. The blast blew windows out of buildings and houses for 3 blocks in all directions.

I was knocked unconscious when the door struck me from behind, and I landed on a worktable face down, then rolled off and fell **on my face onto the floor, (sound familiar) 'the incident with the dentist! ? Luckily, I only received a few broken bones, lumps, bruises and another broken nose. As I lay there unconscious, everything was pitch dark as if I had gone blind.

If you have ever been out in the deep woods on a very dark night with no moonlight to see by, then you have some idea of how dark everything appeared to me. I had the sensation that I was going down through a tunnel, when I came out the other end I saw a bright glow and figures off in the distance. And at that point I heard someone yelling my name. I 'came to' trying to figure out what had happened and then crawled out into the main aisle where I saw one of my co-workers calling for me and then I passed out again.

This was my first dark tunnel experience. Every day I ask GOD, why was I spared and the other 9 taken? Ever since the accident, I have had an over powering feeling that there is something I am supposed to do or complete before I can go to the 'LIGHT'.

After breaking my nose so many times, the inside of my nose has become very distorted and enlarged. Doctors have told me this condition is called a 'deviated septum'. I have a great deal of trouble trying to sleep at night as I cannot breathe through my nose very easily.

At one time I tried to fix the problem and went to see an eye, nose and throat specialist. He recognized my problem immediately and said, "I can shrink your enlarged septum with either a spray or with an injection". He told me I could spray inside my nose 3 times a day and the deviated septum would shrink after about 14 weeks. He told me, "If you want, I can give you an injection that will shrink it in about 1 week". So, I opted for the injection. When the doctor stuck the needle deep inside both sides of my nostrils, I immediately went blind in my left eye, became nauseated, dizzy and started a nosebleed that dumped about a cup of blood all over me, his floor and his chair. I passed out, (for how long I don't know) and when I came to, it took about 3 hours to get my sight back in my left eye. I had to call a couple friends to come and take me and my car home.

So, if I may impart a few words of wisdom to those of you with a deviated septum-do not let your doctor stick a needle into your nose for any reason. My deviated septum is still with me and just as large as ever and will remain with me for as long as I live.

One phenomenon that came out of my near death experience is: Every day, people that I meet at Church, the swap meet, grocery store or where ever pay no attention to me whatsoever. After much meditation and past life regression,

I have come to the conclusion that I should have died in the oven explosion back in 1951 at the age of 19, and been reborn in 1954 and lived a totally different life. So, I am 'off track' and don't exist nor do I belong in this time and space. I call this bizarre.

The "dark tunnel" mystery has kept me awake many nights trying to figure out what the 'tunnel' could be. I would wake up at 3:00 AM and sit on the edge of my bed for an hour or more thinking about it. One morning, (after the passing of many years), just as if God plopped it into my head, there it was. It's not a tunnel at all. We, as 'spirit beings', (I've been told) reside about 2 inches behind our eyeballs. Our senses, (i.e.: sight, sound, touch, smell and taste) are sent over our nerve lines to a point at our brain in the form of electronic frequencies.

We as spirits sense those frequencies at that spot in our brain and determine what our body is seeing, hearing, smelling, feeling and tasting. From early childhood, we learn to associate these frequencies with their sources. As we grow, we learn to recognize sounds, sights, odors, etc. Our eyes can only detect certain wavelengths and frequencies, and we, as spirits can (normally), only 'see' the frequencies "sights" sent to our brains by our eyes. That is the reason we cannot 'see' other spirits or the 'LIGHT' of Heaven while in our bodies.

The frequency of the 'LIGHT' and the frequency of spirits are such that we cannot 'see' them with our eyes. We, as spirits, when outside of our bodies, (exterior), can sense ALL frequencies direct, without the use of our physical body sensors. I believe some people call traveling outside of the body, 'ASTRO' traveling.

Anyway I am straying away from the subject of tunnels. When our body dies or goes through a great trauma and we decide it's no longer feasible to remain in the body, we vacate our body and lose contact with the input sensor frequencies that exist there at the point in our brain where all our sensor inputs arrive. You must learn all over 'again' how to sense electronic frequencies direct, (as a spirit) 'from their sources'. If you have a difficult time regaining this ability, you may not 'see' anything when you first leave your body.

It will be much like being in a basement with no windows or doors, where you couldn't see your hand in front of your face even if you still had a hand. After a bit of time of straining to see again, you will break open a small 'hole' of light in the darkness, (this could take from less than a second to several seconds). As you regain the ability to 'sense' light again directly as a spirit, you will see a 'hole' of light grow larger in front of you until all the darkness disappears. This is what gives people the feeling of going through a tunnel.

After you fully regain your sensing abilities 'again', you will find you can "see" the frequency of the "LIGHT" of Heaven along with the spirits who reside there. One phenomenon you will encounter when you go exterior to your body is the ability to sense in all directions simultaneously. If you have ever seen the Circle-Rama theatre at Disneyland in California, you will have a small understanding of what it is like to be able to view everything in a 360 degree circle, all about you, _all_ at the same moment.

While in your body, your eyes automatically limit your peripheral view, but when outside your body, you must take responsibility for controlling the width of the area you wish to view. I have a few acquaintances who believe the LIGHT of Heaven is made from the collective AURA, (frequency of light) of the spirits that reside there. Our Lord did say that He was the 'LIGHT', but did He mean, He was the Light on the path to Heaven, or did He actually mean He _was_ the 'LIGHT' of Heaven.

I think this may be the beginning of many lengthy, heated discussions. I will attempt to start one of the discussions with the following input. You will take all your memories with you when you go to the 'LIGHT', (If you go to the light).

One thing you may encounter is that when you arrive you may find that other beings are able to 'read' your thoughts AND your memories too. So, all I can say is, unless you have no conscience whatsoever, you may want to 'clean' up your act before you go there.

No one will have to ask, 'what are you doing to me I don't know about. They will instantly know. Also, you will take all your memories with you. Otherwise, "how will you recognize all your friends and family members that are there waiting for you"?

In this paragraph, I would like to go off into the realm of, "I've been told" and "These are just theories for your reading enjoyment". Hold on to your seats, this may be the part where you quit reading and put my book up on a high dark shelf in your library, (Or file it in the round file).

I think we can all agree that we have evil people here among us on this mud ball called Earth. I've been told, each of these people became evil for a reason.

It doesn't just "happen". The problem being is, when a 'person' is evil, we are actually dealing with an evil spirit, and furthermore they at one time, decided to be 'evil'. I believe that we have all had many past lives. I have regressed back many hundreds of years into my past lives. What I experienced during those years has had a great influence over my present personality. A typical example was my Mother always telling me to be "a good boy" or my Dad would get mad and leave us.

My Father died 10 days before my 4th birthday and no one bothered to explain what had happened to him or where he had gone. In my little pea brain, I assumed Dad got mad and left us because I wasn't a good boy. Carry that around with you for 30 years and see what kind of person you decide to be. I spent those 30 years unknowingly trying to find a way to get my Father to come back home.

I wouldn't fight in school, even to defend myself because if I did I would be driving my Father even further away. I unlocked that one at the age of 35 while in a regression session.

The list of different possible scenarios that could cause one to be good (or evil) is endless. My 'caution' to you is; an evil spirit, whether in or out of their body, continue being evil "until" they decide to be otherwise, and they can cause you harm, (while you are out of your body) if you do not know how to escape or control them.

The trick is very simple; the way to travel or escape harm is just 'wish to be somewhere else'. You don't have to know where a person is if you want to be with them. Just wish to be with them and 'zip', there you are.

Our Government, (at all levels) seems to have a very difficult time controlling the people that join and follow in the 'gang' or *group* crime sprees. Don't quote me on this, but I heard on the news that there were at least 20 thousand gangs in the United States. I would like to get on my soap box for just a few lines.

When terrorists involved in a crime are caught and dealt with, any terrorist proven to have been connected in any way with those who committed the crime are hunted down and brought to justice.

Channel 2 Eye Witness News, here in Southern California did a special on drug pushers and prostitutes. The cameraman put a hidden camera in his car and exposed pushers and prostitutes right on the main streets of Hollywood.

So, here's my suggestion: why don't we hire the news media people to locate the drug pushers, prostitutes and gang members and let the police follow them and make the arrests?

The news media could probably locate prostitution rings, drug rings and street gangs and clean up crime in our country in no time at all. As far as street gangs are concerned, we could do one thing that might put an end to street gangs in a short time.

Our legislators could create a new law stating that if any one member of a street gang commits a crime, all members of the gang will be convicted of that same crime and share the same punishment regardless of where they were or what they were doing at the moment of the crime.

In other words, treat them for what they are, terrorists! Young people have choices, and I for one believe they make the decision to do criminal acts. I don't think it matters whether it stems from peer pressure or just for the 'fun' of it.

If this law was on the books, I don't think too many half-hearted potential gang members would be in such a hurry to join a gang. (Of course, the system would have to be willing to carry out the punishments).

Speaking of punishments, if you inform all gang members of what will happen to them if they continue their life of crime, and they continue anyway, when they are caught, whatever they receive is not called punishment. It's called consequences.

End of soap box lecture.

Should you fear death? You should fear it only as much, (or as little) as you fear living. Remember one thing if you remember nothing else. When an evil person, (spirit) leaves their body at death, sometimes they do not stop being evil. So, if you fear an evil person here on earth, you might have problems with them if you meet one of them in the spirit world on the way to the LIGHT.

One thing you might keep somewhere in your bag of memories is, "the way to get away from an evil spirit while you are exterior from your body, is: just wish to be somewhere else or with someone else".

You don't have to know where the person is, just wish to be with them. That is the trick for getting out of uncomfortable situations, (or traps) while out of your body. It is also the "Key" to ASTRO traveling. That's how simple it is. If you want to see Paris while roaming around as a spirit, just wish to be there.

Many years ago, a song was written that became one of the most popular gospel songs of all the modern religious songs. Most people who have either sung the song or enjoyed hearing it don't know where it came from or who wrote it. The song is "I saw the LIGHT", (I saw the LIGHT, I saw the LIGHT, No more darkness, no more night).

You may be surprised to learn, the song was written by an alcoholic drug abuser who was probably the most well known and loved country singer of all time. His Wife forced him out of their home, and after that he wandered around the states bouncing from one flophouse to another, canceling more singing engagements than the popular "No show" country star, George Jones.

I am assuming that when he wrote the song he was at a point in his life where he was trying to turn his life around. He finally died on New Year's Eve in 1951, at the ripe old age of 29. He was my all-time favorite country singer and his name was Hank Williams.

Did he get stoned one time too many, exteriorize from his body and actually see the 'LIGHT' of Heaven, or did he just mean that he finally realized that his life

137

was in shambles and needed to be changed. Therein lies another subject for your think tank.

I've come to believe, that while at the LIGHT, you may be given an option to return to Earth and enter an unoccupied unborn fetus (henceforth past lives). The one main problem with this is, I've also been told that if you do take this option, there is a good chance that before you return to Earth you "will" have all your 'conscious' memories erased, (buried so deep in your consciousness you won't have conscious access to them after you return) unless you later find your way to a person or group that can regress you into your past lives.

If some of you are under the assumption that your memories are carried in the meat and bone memory cells in your brain and you lose them when your body dies, you will find this to be untrue. You 'will' take all your memories with you when you leave your body, ("you can take that to the bank").   I warned you this would be a 'bit' bizarre.

But just think for a moment, what about the children that are born autistic with the ability to speak different languages, play the piano without one lesson or easily solve mathematical problems beyond the normal.   I believe these people slipped through the crack, so to speak, and retained a portion of their memories.

Have you ever experienced the feeling that you had done something before, or had been somewhere before.   Have you ever thought that perhaps these are bits of memories from your past lives?   (More fodder for your mental digestive system).

A few years ago I saw a story on television about a very young girl who lived in Italy.   It seems this 5 year old girl kept telling her parents that she was worried about her husband and children.   Her Mother was afraid her Daughter was having mental problems and took her to see their local Priest at the church.

The young girl related the story to the Priest that she had been married with children and she was worried about them.   She gave the Priest her Husband's name, the name of her children and the address where she had lived.   After several days of quizzing the girl they decided to check out her story and took the girl with them to the nearby town she had described.   When they reached the house, it was exactly as she described it, with her Husband, children and all.

The man living there told the girl's family that his Wife had died about 7 years ago and they had been keeping the grave site up and all was well.   The young girl was satisfied that everything was fine with 'her' family and so she, her parents and the Priest went back to her home town.

After Mass the next week the Priest asked the girl how she was doing after the visit with her past Husband and she didn't know what he was talking about.

In another story that aired on television, a young autistic boy living his life in a specially designed basement in his parent's house had a very strange talent. His Grandmother passed away and left her piano to him. His parents had the piano moved into the basement hoping their Son could amuse himself playing on the keys.

After the piano arrived the boy sat on the bench and stared at the keys for about two weeks. His parents were very disappointed that he wasn't touching the keys at all. After about two weeks the parents heard music coming from the basement and when they investigated they found their young Son sitting at the piano and playing classical music as though he had been studying for years.

This next story will be very hard for you to believe, I'm certain, but believe me I have experienced many, much more bizarre situations of my own, and I believe the story I am about to impart to you is factual. Not too long ago a young black man was involved in a horrible car crash. As he lay in his hospital bed he went into a coma.

His story was broadcast and followed by the local TV media. His girlfriend sat beside his bed every day until one day he came out of his coma. The problem was, when he came out of his coma he couldn't speak, use his hands, walk or recognize any of his family or friends. It was as if he woke as a new born baby.

Here is my explanation of what happened to him. The pain and or the futility of his condition caused him, (the spirit) to give up and leave his body. The Doctors were keeping his body alive through artificial means. Another spirit came along, (that should have been searching for a new born baby body) and entered his abandoned body.

This new spirit apparently had his memories erased and should have entered a new born where not being able to speak, use his hands, walk or recognize people would not have been seen as unusual. Why he entered an adult body instead is a mystery to me and I doubt will ever be explained in my lifetime. Bizarre, yes, but it remains a possibility. Do you have a more logical theory?

While I have the thoughts on the surface of my mind, let me tell you of one of my past life episodes and how it caused me to make crazy decisions. I was a village protector back many years ago in a country that had problems with Bengal Tigers killing the villagers.

I have always been an inventor of sorts ever since I can remember, and I came up with what I thought was a fool proof way to catch the Tiger. The people of that era were not allowed to kill tigers; therefore I had to devise a method of catching the tiger without harm to him or me. I made a strong rope and tied it to the limb of a tree just outside the village and made a lasso loop at the free end of the rope. I staked out a goat at the bottom of the tree, made a circle out of the lasso end of the rope.

I placed the lasso end of the rope on the ground around the goat, and then climbed the tree to wait for the Tiger. When I climbed the tree, I saw that my young Son had followed me and was hiding in the tall grass watching and waiting to see me catch the Tiger. I had told him to stay home but he disobeyed me. While I sat in the tree waiting for the tiger, my Son fell asleep.

Just before sundown, the Tiger showed himself. He circled several times before taking the bait. Just as he grabbed the goat by the neck, I pulled as hard as I could on the rope. I caught him just around his chest, behind his front legs.

He dropped the goat and began to flail and thrash about, jerking on the rope and very nearly bouncing me out of the tree. I had to let go of the rope and hold onto to the limb with both hands and my legs to keep from falling. The Tiger was much larger than I was told and I soon found out how strong he was.

My Son awoke and seeing that I had indeed caught the Tiger, began shouting at the other villagers to come and help. When the Tiger heard my Son yelling, he turned and ran toward the direction from where he had first appeared. As the rope became taut, the branch broke and dropped the branch and me to the ground.

I held onto the branch and the Tiger dragged me for several feet then turned on me and sent me to the 'LIGHT'. The crazy decision my reactive mind made from this was: it is way too dangerous to climb trees. Believe it or not, as an adventurous young man, I could never climb trees with my friends. It terrified me to death. I also had a strong desire to learn roping tricks like Will Rogers, (probably to unconsciously learn a better way to catch the next tiger in my life).

That's how the reactive mind works. I have found reactive mind calculations from over 10,000 years ago that are still causing me problems. The subconscious mind remains intact from one lifetime to the next.

I fully believe that "no man shall see the face of GOD nor open the gates of Heaven, lest he be reborn of the spirit". My problem is, I am not satisfied until

I fully understand just exactly what that means and how is it done. As an engineer, I look at being reborn of the spirit from a different viewpoint than most people. When Buddha said, meditate on your source of existence, and you shall know Nirvana, (or something close to that), I think the people of his day assumed he meant the source of their existence was the umbilical cord attached to their Mothers and they sat down and meditated while staring at their belly buttons.

I look upon the two statements as meaning the same thing. Be reborn of the spirit and meditate or find your source of existence seems like the same thing to me. Being reborn of the spirit to me means going back in your memory and remembering when GOD created you as a spirit.

Meditate on your source of existence to me means find out when and where you were created, (as a spirit). I wish Buddha and Jesus would have been just a little more specific. How do you find when you were created as a spirit you ask?

There are many people throughout this world that are working daily to discover the method. I know that while growing up as a Christian, I was always told that confessing your sins, changing your ways and taking the Lord into your heart was, "being reborn of the spirit". I have seen too many people try to do this and fail.

Even television Evangelists and Catholic Priests preaching the Gospel to hundreds of thousands of people, have failed miserably at it. For myself, the risk of not finding Nirvana, or seeing the face of GOD, pushes me on to a need to cover all the possibilities.

I can no longer live with my Mothers premise that by being a "good boy", all will be well.

CHAPTER X Spirits, Soul and Karma

My younger Brother asked me to give a lecture at his church on the subject matter in my book. I told him I would, but on one condition. Do not introduce me to the group. In the beginning of the lecture, I do not want them to know my name nor the fact that we are brothers.

When I began the lecture, I told them that I was there to increase their awareness. I asked them to look around and see if there were any people there that they did not know. These folks had been meeting every week for several months, some for years, and as they looked around at each other they all agreed that they knew everyone there. So, I asked "What about me, do you all know who I am"? No one knew who I was.

OK, there you go; I have just increased your awareness.

Over the past 45 years I have asked hundreds of people, "Do you have a spirit"? The majority of the answers were, "Of course". Being a mischievous person, I thoroughly enjoyed what was to follow. My next statement to them was, "I can prove that you do not have a spirit, and further more you will freely agree with me".

This is a good time to make sure you have a captured audience, as most will bolt away from you as if you were Lucifer himself. Now that I had their attention, it was time to ask the do you, or don't you, 'Have a spirit' question. When I asked the group, how many of you believe you have a spirit and asked for a show of hands, everyone eagerly raised their hands. I then asked one young man to look out the window and find a tree.

After he had located a tree, I asked him, "If that tree could talk, would it tell you, I am a tree or I have a tree"?

After some thought, he chided, "I am a tree". After thanking him for his response, I asked another person to find a bush. After he located a bush, I asked him, "If that bush could talk, would it tell you I am a bush or I have a bush"?

He immediately responded with, "I am a bush". (Some of you readers may already know where I am going with this, but you will just have to be patient).

I then asked the whole group, "If all you spirits could talk to me through your bodies, would you each say, I am a spirit or I have a spirit"? The majority of the group agreed with me that they 'were' spirits and did not 'have' a spirit.

Ok, you can stop 'booing' me now and get on with the book.

Many people go around saying, "I have a spirit" and don't realize that when they say "I", they are referring to themselves, the 'spirit'; even though they are trapped in a body they 'are' the 'I'-the spirit. When their body finally gives up and stops functioning, and they get popped out of their heads and have to face the fact they are no longer in their body, I am fairly certain the first thoughts they will have is "what happened, and where the h___ am I-I-I-I-I.............The operative word here being "I".

As a spirit, you all have a potential power greater than you could ever imagine. Our Lord said, "You shall do these things and even more". I remember one time when I was exterior, (out of my body). Colors were in vivid Technicolor all around me. I felt, there was not a problem in the world I could not solve.

One thing that is slightly difficult to control is how you sense your surroundings. The feeling you get is a bit like car sickness or sea sickness. I know, you don't have a body so how can you feel sick to your stomach? (That's a good question, someone please go exterior and check it out for me. I'll put your answers in my next book).

That's my way of saying, "Darned if I know".

I do know you can HEAR, SMELL, SEE and maybe taste and feel while outside your body. I've been told that as a spirit, you can travel great distances in the time it takes to decide where you want to be. If you have ever had dreams of flying through the air in your body while you are actually deep asleep in your bed, it is quite possible you were 'ASTRO' traveling.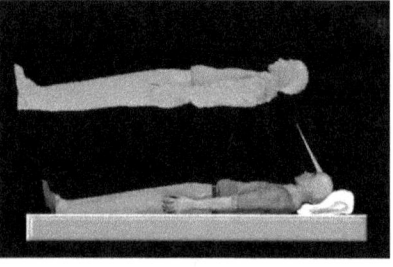

It's much like walking in your sleep, only without your body.

Many times I have caught sight of a movement or an outline of someone out of the side of my eye while watching TV or reading a good book. When I turned my head to look more closely, there was no one there.

I wasn't about to broadcast to all my friends and family that I was 'seeing things', but I just couldn't let it go by. It was happening too many times to be comfortable. As I pushed to try and make it happen on purpose, I found it happened less and less.

As an Engineer, this really set me aback. I had made up my mind I was being visited by ghosts and I wanted to see one full on. However, the harder I tried, the less successful I became.

So, I gave up trying to make it happen, (which wasn't that easy to do either), it's like trying to not think about an elephant just after you tell yourself: *'don't think about an elephant'*. Another thing that bothered me was, every once in a while, (out of the side of my eye) I would see a little spider or bug crawling on the floor. When I turned my head to look directly at the bug, NO BUG! As an engineer, I figured I really had a tough problem to solve.

As a person, I thought I was going off the deep end. It was time for the engineer to get to work. I know it is possible for one spirit to see, (sense) another spirit. This includes the spirits of animals, bugs, etc. I know, we as spirits, reside somewhere behind our eyeballs. It then came to me that when I see people or animals or bugs that aren't really there in the flesh, I must not be seeing them with my eyes.

Every spirit residing in a body has the ability to sense frequencies right through their bodies, (bone, flesh and all). What was happening to me was, I was going exterior from my body just slightly, and sensing the spirits that were around me. What I am saying is, I was not turning my head to look, nor using my eyes to see with.

I was sensing the frequency of the 'spirit beings' directly while being slightly outside my body. If this happens to you, fight the urge to turn and look, just wave your hand at the being in a gesture to show them that you are aware of them.

Doing this also lessons the need to turn and look.

After my eldest Daughter passed due to lung cancer in 2009, (from heavy cigarette use) I saw her in a white flowing gown dancing and twirling off in the distance in our front room. She broke her hip years before and had it replaced twice and could hardly walk without the use of a walker. My Wife passed on 10/11/2012 and she has visited me several times since.

In the middle of the night my senses would wake me and there she would be, standing over me with a smile on her face. This happened three times. The fourth time she appeared, there were two other grey haired women with her, but they didn't stay long enough for me to recognize the other two.

145

When you leave your body, (exteriorize) you will be amazed at how many spirits are roaming around. Some are lost and don't know what to do or where to go, and some are enjoying themselves traveling around seeing the sights. When you go exterior, you will pretty much be on your own.

Depending upon your will power to resist the instincts God stuck you with, (go to the LIGHT, get your memories erased and go back down to Earth and pick up another life) or if you have enough will power, travel the world or the universes and be blown away with what you find. Good luck.

After the millions, perhaps billions of years you have lived in one physical form or another, imagine how many pictures and scenarios you have recorded in your reactive and conscious memories.

My digital camera memory card can hold 143 high quality photographs before it runs out of space and this takes 64 million bytes of data space.

Let's say it takes 8 bytes of data to create one black and white letter of the alphabet. Now take a look at 'your' memory. If your physical visual senses are working properly, every day you record, in color, super high quality and super high speed, everything that happens to you during your waking hours, (and in your dreams while you are sleeping). This is high quality, color video.

My camera takes color 'still' photographs only. You record high color video movies in your memory every day of your life and seem to never run out of memory.

It can be proven to you that you still have, recorded in your memory, incidents that happened during all your many, many past lives. If I do nothing more than get you to think about or hopefully search into your own past lives, I have achieved one of my goals.

So, hopefully we agree that you 'are' a spirit, and that you don't 'have' a spirit, right? Now if you told me you 'have' soul, I might be inclined to agree with you. To me 'soul' is the accumulation of all the good thoughts, good experiences, good deeds, talents, etc. you have accomplished in your life. It is expressed through your personality.

Many people use the word Karma without the faintest clue of what it is, how they attain it or how it actually affects them. I'm not sure that anyone really knows exactly what Karma consists of, how it is created or how it affects the human being, (including yours truly).

I would like to take a crack at explaining my definition of the word. I am by habit, very long winded, so put on your patience hat if you haven't already done so.

The simple explanation I have been hearing is: Karma is the accumulation of all the anti-survival acts a person has committed, (objective and subjective) against others. Others can include: any other living person/s, animal/s, living things and quite possibly inanimate objects.

The human being has a driving need to be right, 'all the time' and when they commit an anti-survival act against others, there comes a strong need to justify their wrongful deed.

If this is not possible, the person may pull in a form of punishment upon themselves at some later date, or lifetime, (depending on the severity of the deed). To me pulling in punishment on yourself is a major part of the definition of Karma.

Be assured of one thing, you will take all your memories with you when you leave your body. One piece of evidence to this is the fact that almost all the people that have had a near death experience and go to the 'LIGHT' and then return back to their body, almost always recount the story that they saw, deceased loved ones standing there waiting for them.

If their memories were lost in the dead meat brain back in their body, how did they recognize their loved ones who were waiting for them at the 'LIGHT'?

Don't take my word for all this.

Get on your steady steed and search for your own truths wherever they may take you and down whatever path you find.

GOOD LUCK, GOD Speed and SEE YOU AT THE 'LIGHT'.

CHAPTER XI
A Letter to My Granddaughters

Dearest Granddaughter,

I am hoping I can impress upon you the seriousness of my words. I have been patiently waiting for many years for you to come to a point in your life where you have a genuine need to heed them. I studied the ways of the Jedi for many years, but your Grandmother couldn't accept my studies and did not want me to continue. The whole family sided with her and to save my marriage, I stopped my training many years ago. Most of my abilities have left me now, but I still have the ability to teach and guide those who wish to follow the ways of the Jedi.

As far as I know everyone has one or more Jedi protectors, (Guardian Angels) that follow them around and do their best to keep them safe. My Jedi protectors became very upset with me because I gave up my studies. You see, they learn as you learn and they become very excited as you achieve more and more knowledge and abilities. So, speak to them out loud when you have the opportunities.

They love to be recognized and acknowledged. To give you a little perspective on them, people who smoke, drink alcohol, curse like drunken sailors or do drugs on a daily basis have a very hard time as they get older. Most people think the ailments they acquire are from the vices they enjoyed. Not entirely true, most Jedi protectors do not like these vices and will abandon you to your fate, and without them helping to take care of your bodily functions-too bad so sad. Break one of the 10 commandments and you would probably have to get down on your knees for a month and beg for them to come back.

Also, don't make bold statements, (postulates) about how you are going to gain new abilities, lose weight, become a better person, etc. that you don't intend to keep. If you do, your Jedi's will sit back and say "OK, have at it and good luck", and perhaps they will laugh a little when and if you fail miserably. Break direct promises to them, and they will drop you like a hot potato and leave you to your own suffering again.

But, if you acknowledge their existence and ask them out loud to please help you do this or that, you will get an entirely different outcome. They will be your conscience and when you stray, you will hear them say, "What will you miss the most, us or that candy bar you are drooling over".

When you make a postulate, don't put conditions on it, just aim for the final result you want. Your Great Grandpa had a secretary that was not loyal to him at all, and stuck it to him every chance she got. Great Grandma told me about her and I could see they did not know what to do about it. I told Grandma that we could postulate her leaving, and Great Grandma said, "Oh no, I don't want her to suffer". I told her, "No, we won't put any bad conditions on it; she will find her own reason for leaving". Great Grandma said, "OK, how do we do it"? "We just did", I replied. Three days later Great Grandma called me and said, "The Secretary called me and was so happy, she is pregnant and wants to go home and be a stay at home Mom. I said, "Thank you God and my Jedi's".

I cannot take you to the level of full Jedi Master, but you can continue with my Jedi friend who can. Without naming names, I think you know who I mean. I am so happy that you have stars in your eyes finally. All I have left are tears of regret. I am patiently waiting for your younger Sister to reach her need also. Hopefully she will someday. If I am not around I hope you will be able to be there for her.

Never lose sight of the fact that evil exists here on Earth all around us. Where is it, and how does it affect mankind? I'll try to give you a summary. There are evil Jedi protectors that follow people like drug dealers, evil dictators, suppressive type A people, etc. They love creating evil and influence people in any way they can.

An example of someone who got stuck with evil Jedi's is Charlie Sheen. He went through hell while all along believing he was 'winning'. A Jedi on the level of Darth Vader is working overtime trying to take over Earth His influence in Syria, Iran, North Korea and Pakistan to name a few, is very strong. The end result of his activity is death and destruction, however he doesn't allow his subjects to see this until it is too late.

This evil Jedi influence over people is the very reason the Lord said, "Forgive them, for they no not what they do". The people are not aware that they are being manipulated by evil Jedi's, and the Jedi's are not aware that they have been manipulated by someone on the level of Darth Vader.

A good example of people who have very powerful Jedi's would be people Like Ellen DeGeneres, Oprah, or any one of the original astronauts. The host of the Wheel of Fortune show is another. Pat is extremely polite to the contestants, and the winners are usually bright eyed people, with bubbly personalities.

Once you have tried a few times, you will be able to spot the people who live without help from their Jedi's; you can see it in their faces.

THE HUGE DIFFERENCE IS MADE WHEN A PERSON RECOGNIZES THAT THEY HAVE JEDI PROTECTORS AND ACKNOWLEDGES THEM, USES THEIR HELP, AND THANKS THEM FOR THEIR PATIENCE AND HELP.

This makes all the difference in the World. This is when you will connect with God within you and peace, love and power will come to you. Oh, how I miss my Jedi's.

I will begin my lecture with the Properties of the Conscious Mind. One thing that really bugs me is when people say things like: "My mind did this or my mind did that". It is really ridiculous to think that the pictures of your memories can do something all on their own. Never going to happen-take that to the bank.

The only one doing anything is you, the SPIRIT. You record everything around you the whole time you are awake, in full Technicolor, highest resolution available, Stereo Hi Fidelity Sound, In full focus at any distance, (if your eyeballs and ears are working properly) and you NEVER run out of memory space! You even record your dreams when you are sleeping.

Amazing when you sit and ponder how large a hard drive would have to be to record my 82 years here on this mud ball called earth. It is called the Conscious mind because it is recorded primarily while you are awake and you can, (if you are not somehow physically impaired) access the pictures therein with somewhat ease. Not too many people ponder these thoughts but, if you are in present time and really try, don't picture a green elephant with pink ears.

I said, "Don't think about a green elephant with pink ears". Did you think of one? It was pretty hard not to huh? But, did you know that for most people it is impossible to bring up pictures of two different things at the same time? Try it. Therefore, if you come up with a negative though, just quickly say out loud, "erase that thought please" then replace it with a positive postulate.

Your Jedi protectors don't realize that you don't want everything that comes out of your mouth, (postulating) and they just may produce it for you anyway. You really need to be careful, even with your smallest thoughts. They are like sticks of dynamite waiting to be lit. The ways of the Jedi may be considered complex and difficult, however the rewards are greater than you could ever imagine.

Con=with and Scio's= awareness. These conscious memory pictures alone don't have much power over you other than to influence your future decisions if you recall them. Or they can evoke emotions when you access them, such as tears, laughter, etc. The subconscious mind is a 'horse of a different color', (I've always wanted to use that in a sentence).

The reactive, (subconscious) mind has to have three conditions present in order to begin recording. You must be unconscious to some degree, anywhere from feeling woozy to flat out unconscious, you must have fear for your survival, for an imagined fear), and you must have some pain present. (It could be emotional or physical pain). When those three conditions are present, your subconscious mind will begin recording with the same clarity as the conscious mind. There exists a great difference between the two though. The reactive mind can have a great effect upon you. When I was born, the Doctor placed a metal band with a built-in handle around my head so he could pull me out.

The pain, fear and unconsciousness were certainly present and my reactive mind recorded it all. At the young age of 14, I took all my lawn mowing money and hired a local golf pro to teach me the art of golf. When we finally got out on the course, I ended up sick. It was because I pulled my hat down tightly onto my head and the reactive mind thought I had the clamp back.

You see, the reactive mind didn't see the difference between the cap and the clamp. It does not register differences, it only sees similarities. If it feels similar, it believes it's the same. If it sounds similar, it believes it's the same. If it smells similar, it believes it's the same. If it looks similar, it believes it's the same. Are you getting the gist of it yet? It gave me all the symptoms of being born all over again.

It's like if you were attacked by an Eagle for several minutes, (lots of blood, cuts and bruises, and later in your life your aunts parrot flew onto your shoulder, you would probably freak out and faint dead away. The similarity, 'feathers, wings, flight, claws, etc.' (A=A=A). Think of some things that scare you or make you queasy and there is probably a reactive mind recording of a past trauma there.

Once you go back, (regression) and review these events you will null and void these recordings and they will transfer over into your conscious mind and then they will have no control over you any longer.

A few disembodied spirits have some of the powers of a Jedi Knight. They can move objects, make themselves partially visible, make noises, create problems for you, (postulates) etc. etc. Your Uncle Mel brought the odor of cigarettes into my house about a week after he passed. I think he came to me for answers that I didn't have for him. I verbally told him that I knew he was there and I told him to go to the Light.

As for your constant problems, remember, problems don't grow out on the pavement or in your garden. They have to be created by someone and to end the constant problem syndrome you need to find the creator/s and stop them. (Remember, you are one of the suspects). During your session part of the studies, you will go through a process that will stop you from 'pulling' problems in on yourself.

About now you are probably saying to yourself, "If my Grandpa went through all this, why does he still have problems?" The answer to that is: 'If you don't use it, you will lose it'.

Read on and pay attention. Your Father creates problems in his head constantly. 'We will go broke and lose everything' is his favorite one, even though after believing this EVERY DAY for years, it hasn't happened yet. He was trained in the art of negative postulates by the Prince of darkness, 'Darth Vader' and has no control over his affliction what-so-ever. Unfortunately for you, you were trained by your Father so, 'Guess what Princess'. You have gone into agreement with his negative postulates one too many times. To sum up all his negative thoughts into one sentence is easily done: "you will FAIL before you've even begun'.

As you become more proficient at making postulates work, your Jedi protectors will come back to you and postulate with you. Like me, your Jedi protectors have been waiting for many long years for this day. They will do their best to keep you and your Family safe. Like, sometimes when you miss your off ramp, turn off on the wrong street, have a flat tire, breakdown, etc. etc. it is because they see something harmful on your current path and it's the only way they have to divert you from your course. (You don't understand why things happen because you haven't learned yet how to pay attention to them and communicate with them). If you are squeamish about having these spirits around you-you had better toughen up, because when you start this journey you will no doubt become very aware of them.

Their usual way of letting you know they are there is by sending cool or cold air around you. I have always known the Force was strong in you and your Sister. If you follow the path of the Jedi, you will feel its force for sure one day.

Here are some ways you can practice your postulates without causing harm to others. 'When you are standing in line at the market, say hello to the person in front of you, get their attention, and say to yourself, " You should let this young girl go ahead of you, she has two small children and you aren't in any hurry".

If the person has a brain and one or two Jedi protectors, she will most likely turn to you and let you go ahead of her. I was on the freeway coming home from classes and my Jedi protectors put the picture in my head of a blowout. I knew my tires were bald and without thinking I said out loud, "Oh no, give it to someone else". And immediately, BANG! The car next to me had a blowout. I thought oh damn; I'd better not use that solution again. I apologized out loud to the other driver and went on my way.

The ways of the Jedi are very powerful. If you remain true to them, they will take good care of you.

I don't see how GOD can grant all the prayers that come to him. Can you picture one billion people praying to Him sometimes three times a day? Wow. And most prayers are hitting him simultaneously, and unfortunately most go unanswered.

"Whenever three or more gather in my name, I will be there".

How many people are meeting in His name simultaneously at every Christian church in the World just on a Sunday? How does he show up at all those places at the same time? That's another clue to me that GOD is in everyone everywhere and the idea that you can make use of the GOD within you and cause things to happen is true. So, to me it stands to reason that if you can get two or more people to agree with your postulate, your chances of being successful are much better than postulating alone.

Some people had Jedi protectors that were so powerful many of their postulates came true even when predicted far in the future. (Nostradamus for one) When the California weatherman comes on Television and predicts rain for Super Bowl Sunday and two million Californians say he's wrong and it doesn't rain, he is left scratching his head and wondering what happened. (Mass postulates happened, that's what).

Whatever the mass population agrees upon is usually what will happen. The Mayan calendar ending at 2012 means the world is coming to an end then. The hole in the stratosphere is causing global warming. Nostradamus was unable to see anything past the year 2000. World war three will be here soon. An earthquake will dump California into the ocean, Tornados occur in Kansas, It rains 24/7 in Washington and Oregon, Armageddon is just around the corner, And the very best one, is "If you don't use it, you will lose it". Ha Ha. Oh! Wait, that last one is true.

All I can say is, "Please stop agreeing with all these terrible postulates".

Once you begin your training, there is no quitting as I did for your Grandmother's sake 46 years ago. It's the path of a lifetime. You will need to teach your children the ways of the Jedi. Watch George Lucas's movies Star Wars and wonder with me how George tapped into his past lifetime memories and remembered what happened "Long Ago and Far Away". The Jedi's existed long ago and far away.

How many Jedi's are still around and roaming the universe-who knows?

Your children may have to reach the ages of 12-15 before they can comprehend your ways. However, you can prepare them by learning to keep negative postulates from being forced upon them, or even spoken around them. Think this will be easy? Think again. (Negative postulate-ha ha) You have always made learning easy.

How do postulates/prayers work? I guess each of us have an idea how prayers work. Most of us pray like crazy when we get in trouble. When you get older and your children never come to see you unless they need money or your help, then you might get some idea how God feels when you pray only on special need occasions. Ever wonder how GOD keeps track of all the prayers that come to him every day from all parts of the World? If you believe life exists on other planets and in other Universes and they are also praying to one GOD, then it becomes mind boggling. That is way too much for my pea brain to understand. As for postulates, it all boils down to the old adage, you have to believe it to see it.

Postulate:

- Verb: Accept or suggest the existence, fact, or truth of something as a basis for reasoning, discussion, or belief.

- Noun: A thing suggested or assumed as true as the basis for reasoning, discussion, or belief.

So, in order to postulate something into existence, you must first believe it is already possible. To 'postulate' to me, means: using the power of GOD that is within you to create something or a condition or event that you need to have happen. Usually when you postulate, you automatically come up with a counter-postulate that neutralizes your original postulate. This is one of the major reasons people give up so easily and stop believing in postulates/prayers.

So, seriously, call upon your Jedi Knights for help and use the Power within you to create for yourself and your Family the life you deserve. If postulates didn't exist and didn't work, why in the World did Webster include the word in his dictionary? Making postulates stick requires first that you believe that the Force (GOD) is within you and you can tap into that power and use it for good and against evil.

But, without evil to combat, we would be a very mundane society. Under perfect conditions with no evil present, someone would ask you, "How are you today" and your answer would probably be, "Oh, same as yesterday, I snapped my fingers and created another billion dollars". You need to fail from time to time to keep you humble and in awe of GOD's greatness.

Should you go to the Light when you leave your body at death? For me this is a toss of the coin. I really don't have enough experience on the subject to even suggest one way or the other.

My very wise Jedi Master Friend says 'no' don't go there. My friend tells me the Light was created by or is under the control of beings my friend calls 'implanters'. These implanters are apparently able to activate your sub-conscious mind and place pictures, thoughts, ideas, concepts, fears and etc. into your sub-conscious mind. This I understand is a method of controlling you and getting you to do things you normally wouldn't do. This is a deeper but similar method of hypnotism.

I don't know exactly how it's done, however in my many hours of regression sessions, (1200 hours) I have seen many events that were created in my sub-conscious memories that were not created by me.

I do know that if you go to the Light, you will take all your memories of your last lifetime with you. However, the urge to return to Earth and begin a new life there is very strong in many beings, and if you choose to return, your conscious memories will be erased.

I don't think this is totally effective like 100% with some beings as they retain some of their skills and some of their strong desires from their last life. This is why some autistic children are able to speak different languages, play the piano, sing opera or tell you stories of their past lifetimes.

Speaking of strong desires, there is one that we should discuss here. 'This is the desire to live your life as a male or female'. This desire is second only to the desire to live again.

As an example: when a young girl is growing up, she plays house and plays at cooking, preparing for the day when she becomes old enough to get married and be a homemaker for real. In too many cases, usually at an early age, she possibly gets abducted, raped and killed. Then, off she goes to the Light. She decides to try again and finds her way into another female unborn body. All goes well until she somehow, (it's never been revealed to me as to why this happens) she will pull in another abduction, rape and death upon herself.

This, to say the least, is very frustrating.

She has been cut off twice, (sometimes more often) from becoming a Wife, Mother and Homemaker. However, she will continue to keep trying and during one of her attempts she will accidently enter a male body. This brings about a few different alternatives. If she realizes what has happened she could terminate her life. (Doctors call it 'crib death'). I have real experience in this aspect of life.

My Mother first had my older Brother, (8 years older than I) and then two years before she had me, she had a little girl. That was ME also. However, I hated the idea of growing up as a girl, (I'm talking HATE here) SO I DID THE CRIB DEATH THING.

I know you and everyone else will ask: How do you know all this? When you go through your training sessions you will learn these things for yourself and much, much, much more. All others will have to take my word for it or just suffer in disbelief and cycle from lifetime to lifetime. Anyhow, I stray from my point.

When she finds herself in a male body, she could just continue on, unaware of her folly and grow up with a few female traits and live a fairly normal life. Or, she could retain most of her female desires from her past life times and end up turning gay, desiring all the normal goals of a female while living in a male body.

A similar situation can happen with beings who hate the idea of living as a female and accidently get born into a female body, therefore becoming a Lesbian. Mystery solved!

I have over 1500 one hour taped lectures by the Jedi Master. I also have 15 to 20 of his books and several of his study course materials. I was never very good at performing sessions on another person or on myself for that matter, (solo sessions).

I was always afraid that I would do something wrong and screw someone up. I never got enough practice in, to hone my skills before I had to quit.

Just like the, 'You will fail before you begin thing'. I have a postulate that someday I will return to my studies and become the Jedi Master I have always wanted to be.

Before the end of this year, I will have my tapes organized and sorted out, and you can listen to them and study. Studying is only half the battle, you will have to meet someday with my Jedi Master friend and do some sessions.

That's when the World opens up, sparks fly and you will gain abilities far beyond your imagination.

And you will know the truth, and the truth will make you free
John 8:32

The TRUTH shall set you free.

I love you more than time allows,

Grandpa.

www.ingramcontent.com/pod-product-compliance
Lightning Source LLC
Chambersburg PA
CBHW070912290526
45795CB00001B/299